Prosper

A Guide to Flourishing in Life, Business, and Career

Compiled by

Sharvette Mitchell

Sonya Chiles • Ifedayo "Dayo" Greenway
Yolanda Hall • Maya Harris • Tanya Russell
Jean Tillery • Euronda Travis • Wanda Washington
Sandy Weekes • Bishop Gale LeGrand Williams

Mitchell Productions, LLC

Prosper

Paperback ISBN# 979-8-9876197-5-9
Hardback ISBN# 979-8-9876197-6-6
eBook ISBN# 979-8-9876197-7-3

Published by:
Mitchell Productions, LLC
www.Mitchell-Productions.com

Back Cover Photography
Kimie James

Anthology Editor
Chandra Sparks Splond, M.S.E.
www.chandrasparkssplond.com

Book Design by Brand It Beautifully™
www.branditbeautifully.com

Contents

For the person who dared to dream, and for those who are just beginning to dream—this book is a testament to the strength of our collective journey.

*To every person who has ever felt unseen
—this is for you. Together, we rise.*

Introduction

Hello, my friends!

I want to share something with you—a book that speaks to the essence of what it means to thrive in life, business, and career. We've all faced moments where success or growth feels like it's just beyond our grasp. Those times when we're working hard, giving our all, but still wondering if we'll ever reach that next place of fulfillment.

Well, let me tell you, Prosper is the book that will help you shift your mindset. This isn't just another book to put on your bookshelf (side note: I love a good bookshelf; my books are color coded on my bookshelf!). It's a deeply personal journey shared by ten extraordinary women who have walked the road to their level of success with grit, grace, and a whole lot of heart. Through their stories and guidance, they offer you a roadmap to navigate your own prosperous pathway. You will find that we are all more alike than we are different.

Each chapter of Prosper is like a transparent conversation with a friend. In short story form, these authors talk about their struggles, their triumphs, and the lessons they've learned along the way. They give you their perspective, and, most importantly, they give you hope.

This book is your permission slip to prosper—in your bank account, in your spirit, in your relationships, and in your purpose. Whether you're looking to elevate your career, grow your business, or find balance in your personal life, Prosper is one of the tools you need to aide in your growth.

So, open these pages, take in each word, read the chapters in order or out of order and let them inspire you to rise to new heights. Remember, prosperity isn't just about what you achieve; it's about who you become along the way. And my friends, you are destined to flourish.

Welcome to Prosper. *Your journey to thriving begins now.*

Sharvette Mitchell

Visionary Author
Founder of Mitchell Productions

The Platform Builder®, Coach, Speaker and host of The Sharvette Mitchell Radio Show

WOSB, SWaM & NMSDC certified

Elevating Brands, Fueling Success! Boosting Business Growth Through Tailored Solutions for Small Businesses, Corporations and Government Entities.

www.Mitchell-Productions.com

Prospering Is About More Than Money. Prospering Is a Mindset.

Euronda Travis, MS, LPC, LSATP

Ninety-one dollars. That's all it was—my first check as a business owner. A paper check, mind you. And let me tell you, receiving it felt like winning the lottery. I remember holding it in my hands, feeling a sense of pride and validation wash over me. After six months of pouring my heart and soul into my business without seeing a dime, that $91 check was a validation, a glimmer of hope that maybe, just maybe, I could make this entrepreneurial dream a reality. It was a check—a tangible symbol of progress.

I was excited to be able to take it home, share it with my husband who had believed in me when I didn't believe in myself. I called my adult children, excited that I had finally gotten paid. They cheered like it was a million bucks! I remember calling my mother who was initially stunned that $91 could make me this excited. When I broke it down and told her how I hadn't made a dime in six months, she understood and told me how proud she was of me and that $91. I cried and let out an audible sigh. All the pressure of starting a business came running out of my eyes in the form of the biggest tears ever.

Euronda Travis, MS, LPC, LSATP

I'm Euronda Travis, a licensed professional counselor, a licensed substance abuse practitioner, board-approved clinical supervisor, business consultant, therapist, and proud entrepreneur. I am a wife of a super-supportive husband and mother to two amazing adult daughters. Eight years ago, I took the leap and founded Comprehensive Counseling Solutions of Virginia, a behavioral health agency dedicated to serving those in need of mental health care. Since its inception, my agency has touched the lives of thousands, employed more than two hundred individuals, allowed me to give to the charities that are closest to my heart, and afforded me the freedom to chart my own course.

But let me rewind a bit. Back when it all began, I was drowning in debt, self-doubt, and a serious case of imposter syndrome. Despite my passion for entrepreneurship, fear and uncertainty threatened my dreams. I stumbled through those early days, navigating the maze of business ownership with no mentor and no written plan. Let's just say, I made my share of mistakes along the way, and some days my pride got in the way of asking for help. I would not recommend starting this way; however, I know so many entrepreneurs do. What I learned was just to get started. Start scared, but do it anyway. I slowed down, sought out mentors and collaborators. I learned that being the boss didn't mean that I knew everything; it meant that I was responsible for everything, and I had to be okay with that.

During the beginning of my journey, one of my biggest hurdles was overcoming the negative self-talk and limiting beliefs that held me back. I'll admit it, there were moments when I questioned whether I had what it takes to get it done. Despite my training and expertise, I found myself paralyzed by fear of failure. It was as if my mind had become a battleground, with negative thoughts and self-limiting beliefs waging war against my aspirations. I had days when I would just stay in the bed, afraid to take on the day. Deep down, I knew I couldn't let fear dictate my future. I set out to reframe my mindset and silence the inner critic and prosper.

Prospering Is About More Than Money. Prospering Is a Mindset.

I needed to prove myself wrong. I *could* in fact do this! I refused to go back to a job I hated, working for people who refused to see my light, and when they did, they made sure to dim it quickly! I knew that if my spirit was going to survive, I had to succeed at being my own boss. I once said that I felt I was psychologically unemployable. Well, after years of talking to entrepreneurs, I knew that I was not the only one.

So, how was I going to make this work? I took a look at myself and applied techniques that I would use with any client walking into my office with the same issues. Now, my role in writing this chapter is not to be your therapist. Please know that if you are experiencing psychological discomfort and need assistance, that you should reach out to a therapist in your area. Think of this chapter as more of a cautionary tale of detailing my journey.

The purpose of this chapter is to give you a few nuggets and encouragement to set you on your entrepreneurial journey. I truly believe that the world is a better place because of women entrepreneurs, and if you are reading this, that tells me you have an interest in blazing your own path.

As you embark on your entrepreneurial journey, it's easy to get caught up in the logistics of business planning, market research, and financial considerations. While these elements are undoubtedly important, there's one foundational aspect that often goes overlooked: mindset. This is where I find most of us get stuck. I know this was my biggest hurdle, and if you are like I was, this should be where you focus your attention initially. Growing up, my mother always said, "Get your mind right!" She used this whenever I had what I will call, "stinking thinking."

Alright, let's cut to the chase. You're a dynamo, juggling a thousand things at once—mom, wife, employee, aunt, niece, daughter, friend, and so many other things—and eyeing that entrepreneurial dream with a mix of excitement and trepidation. But before you dive headfirst into the world of business plans and market research, there's one thing you need to tackle first: your mindset. Before you can conquer the world, you've got to conquer your own mind.

Without the proper mindset, all your dreams, preparation, and plans will fail. It is important to develop a mindset that will help you secure the bag! Here are a few things you will need to keep in mind.

1. *Believe in Yourself*: Look, if you're going to make it in the wild world of entrepreneurship, you've got to believe in yourself—like, really believe. None of that half-hearted "maybe I can do this" nonsense. We're talking full-on, chest-pounding, "I've got this" confidence. This is key. This is a muscle that you will have to flex often. No more shrinking and playing small. As women, sometimes we are taught to shrink, to fit in to make others comfortable with our light, and I am telling you, it is your time to shine! Get out there and blind them with that light.

2. *Roll with the Punches*: Entrepreneurship is a rollercoaster ride. You'll hit highs, you'll hit lows, and sometimes you'll feel like you're spinning in circles. But hey, that's all part of the adventure. A resilient mindset will help you weather the storms and come out stronger on the other side. While true, this is hard to do. I can't tell you how many days I wanted to throw in the towel because the lows were pretty low. It is important to use adversity as fuel.

3. *Think on Your Feet*: In business, things can change in the blink of an eye. One day you're riding high on the success train, and the next you're scrambling to put out fires. A flexible mindset will help you adapt to whatever curveballs the universe throws your way. Don't be afraid to make decisions. As the boss, making decisions and thinking on your feet is your actual job.

4. *Embrace the Unknown*: Let's face it: Entrepreneurship is a bit like going on a blind date. It's scary, it's thrilling, and it's downright unpredictable. You may not know what is around the corner, but expect it to be amazing. Embrace the uncertainty, and get out there.

5. *Have a Growth Mindset*: Last but not least, we've got to talk about growth mindset. This is not a fixed mindset, where you're stuck in your ways and resistant to change. No, ma'am, we're all about growth around here—constantly learning, evolving, and pushing ourselves to new heights. Knowing that you are not going to be the same person next year that you are today as an entrepreneur is key. You will grow, you will change, and that is a good thing! You have the power to change lives.

So, these are all things I had studied and knew about, but I still had mental hurdles to conquer.

Enter cognitive behavioral therapy (CBT), a powerful tool that would ultimately change the trajectory of my journey. With CBT, I learned to challenge the distorted thinking patterns that were holding me back. I began to recognize the irrationality of my fears and doubts, replacing them with more rational and empowering beliefs. I started to confront my fears head-on, reframing them as opportunities for growth rather than obstacles to be feared. I often think that the largest fear I had was actually a fear of being successful. Once I started to examine where that fear originated, I began to feel more powerful. Each setback became a lesson in resilience, a chance to strengthen my resolve and push forward with renewed determination.

But CBT wasn't just about changing my thoughts. It was also about taking action. I realized that true progress requires more than just positive thinking; it requires concrete steps toward our goals.

It wasn't easy, and there were plenty of bumps in the road. Learning how to handle billing? That was a comedy of errors in itself. I actually had to wait until someone came in for an interview and taught me right on the spot! Needless to say, I hired him, and he taught me a lot. With each setback, I reminded myself that I was capable of doing hard things, a mantra that carries me through each day.

Today, as I reflect on the journey from that $91 check to where I am now, I'm filled with gratitude for the lessons learned and the obstacles overcome. My agency stands as a testament to the power of perseverance and the potential within each of us to thrive against the odds. I don't say this to impress you, but to impress *upon* you that if I can do it, so can you. Today, I help high-achieving women who want to start their own entrepreneur journey overcome mental obstacles by consulting and coaching.

Here are the ten tips I give them:

1. Identify and Challenge Negative Thoughts: Begin by identifying the negative thoughts that arise when contemplating your entrepreneurial journey. Are there recurring doubts or fears that hold you back? Let me tell you, you are not too old, too broke, too inexperienced, and there aren't too many people already doing it. Once identified, challenge these thoughts by asking yourself for evidence that supports or refutes them. This process helps to uncover irrational beliefs and replace them with more rational, empowering ones. I did this at least one hundred times a day. There were times when my mind would wonder and these thoughts would creep in. This is a muscle that you will have to build up in order to prosper. You are allowed and *should* take up space. The world needs what you have to offer!

2. Practice Self-Compassion: As an overworked, high-performing woman, it's crucial to cultivate self-compassion. Acknowledge that starting a business is going to be a challenging journey, and it's okay to feel overwhelmed at times. Treat yourself with kindness and understanding, just as you would a close friend facing a similar situation. I often ask my coaching and consulting clients to find a picture of their younger self. Put it somewhere you can see it daily and have those tender conversations with yourself. Commit to giving her the tenderness that you needed then, and let her know that you guys are doing great. It is okay to be tired and overwhelmed, but if this is your dream, you must not quit on yourself. Your younger self is counting on you, and so are so many others. *You got this!*

3. Set Realistic Goals: Break down your entrepreneurial goals into smaller, achievable tasks. Setting realistic goals helps to prevent feelings of being overwhelmed and fosters a sense of accomplishment as you make progress. Celebrate each milestone along the way, no matter how small. Goals need to be specific and measurable. There is a principle that says the longer you give a person to do something, the longer it will take them to do it. Act with a sense of urgency to get your goals accomplished. Do not negotiate with yourself. The decision to prosper is an urgent one, and there should be nothing that you let get in between you and your goal. No excuses! You should treat your goals seriously and review them daily. Review your daily activity and make sure that you do an audit of how you spend your time. I missed lots of TV shows, concerts, and get-togethers all in the name of setting up my business, and today, I am glad I took that approach. Anything that is pulling you away from your goal should be minimized until you get your goals met. This is hard, but remember, you can do hard things, and you are worth it.

4. Visualize Success: Use visualization techniques to imagine yourself succeeding in your entrepreneurial venture. Picture yourself confidently overcoming obstacles and achieving your goals. Visualization can help to reprogram your subconscious mind, reinforcing positive beliefs about your capabilities. Write out your success story. I call this beginning with the end in mind. The story needs to be as specific as possible. I knew that I wanted an office on this street, with a certain size staff offering specific services, and I even visualized my lifestyle as a result of the business. I cut out pictures, I saw myself in my office with clients and a full appointment book. Today, my vision of success looks different, and yours will change over time, but start to dream about what it would be like if you actually stepped out on faith, used your gifts, and walked in the direction of your dreams. Most of the time, this is the hardest thing for my clients to do. Dreaming has become a thing of the past, due to the stress and structure of our everyday life. What would you be doing if you knew failure was not an option? I dreamed of getting to my office every day at ten a.m. because mornings and I don't get along. Now, my first appointment is at ten a.m. daily. It may sound like a small thing, but getting up at six a.m. to make it by 7:30 a.m. to a job I hated was a huge motivator for me. What is your driving reason for wanting to go into business? Visualize in detail what that would look like. Don't be afraid to see yourself winning! Drown out the "what if this, then that" talk. Allow yourself to prosper first in your mind.

5. Challenge Perfectionism: As a high-performing woman, perfectionism is a common trait. However, perfectionism can be paralyzing and hinder progress. Practice embracing imperfection and viewing failures as opportunities for growth. Trust me, failures will come, and that's okay. I have had clients that use perfectionism as a crutch and a reason to delay, delay, delay. I can't say that I have not done this myself. I am actually doing it right now as I edit this chapter for the fifth time. We need to let go of the need to be perfect. There is always going to be room for growth, and nothing is ever perfect, period. (Closes laptop and stops editing.) Remember, done is better than perfect.

6. Practice Mindfulness: Incorporate mindfulness techniques into your daily routine to cultivate awareness of your thoughts and emotions. Mindfulness helps to interrupt the cycle of negative self-talk by allowing you to observe your thoughts without judgment. Techniques such as deep-breathing exercises and body scans can help to ground you in the present moment. Become aware of how your thoughts affect your nervous system.

7. Create Affirmations: Develop affirmations that counteract negative self-talk and reinforce positive beliefs about yourself and your abilities. Repeat these affirmations regularly, particularly when facing challenges or self-doubt. For example, "I am capable and deserving of success" or "I have the resilience to overcome any obstacle." Repeating these affirmations in the mirror is a great way to start your day. I have created an affirmation playlist on my phone with some of the songs I find most empowering. Listening to the words lifts my mood and makes me feel like I can take on the day. Incorporate some affirming activity into each day. If you need a jump-start with this, I have developed affirmation cards you can purchase on my website (www.EurondaTravisCounsulting.com) to help you get started. Remember, *you got this!*

8. Seek Support: Surround yourself with a supportive network of friends, family, or fellow entrepreneurs who believe in your vision and can provide encouragement during difficult times. Don't hesitate to reach out for support when needed, whether it's through mentorship, networking events, or professional counseling.

Now, I say this with a small caveat: Dream stealers are real! Oftentimes those closest to us will deter us from reaching out to grab our goals. Those well-meaning relatives or friends who tell you there are too many risks are really projecting their own fear and inadequacies on to you. Be careful about who you share your vision with and know that these opinions and the "advice" they give you is more about where they are than about you. Sharing that you want to open a business with someone who has never done so may sound like a good idea, but oftentimes, there is nothing to be gained from those conversations. As entrepreneurs, our vision, dreams, and desires are unlike those who are comfortable with the W-2 life. Safety, security, and a steady check are the enemy of an entrepreneur. Seek support, however, protect your dream at all costs! Find your tribe, and count on them for support while trying to build your dream business.

9. Challenge Catastrophic Thinking: When faced with setbacks or obstacles, challenge catastrophic thinking patterns that exaggerate the potential negative outcomes. Instead, adopt a more balanced perspective by considering alternative explanations and potential solutions. Reframe setbacks as learning experiences that contribute to your growth and resilience. This is a "What's the worst thing that could happen?" tip. And the worst thing is usually not so bad. Stop letting anticipated setbacks and obstacles be the reason you don't move forward with your business idea.

10. Take Action Despite Fear: Finally, recognize that fear is a natural part of the entrepreneurial journey, but it doesn't have to dictate your actions. Practice taking small, manageable steps toward your goals, even in the face of fear or uncertainty. Each action you take builds momentum and reinforces your belief in your ability to succeed. Do it, even if you have to do it afraid. Get started, and let the momentum carry you into prosperity. Remember, *you got this!*

By incorporating these CBT techniques into your entrepreneurial journey, you can effectively tackle negative self-talk and limiting beliefs, paving the way for success and fulfillment as a business owner. Remember, you are capable of achieving greatness, and your journey is worthy of celebration every step of the way. Go and take up space! Know that you belong in every room you enter, and better yet, believe that they are waiting for you!

So, to those of you reading this book, trying to navigate the mental hurdles. To anyone who's ever felt the weight of self-doubt bearing down upon them, I offer this advice: Prosper. Decide to prosper. Be dogmatic and unforgiving about your decision to seek out more. Despite the doubts. Despite the setbacks. Despite the naysayers who may try to dim your light.

To anyone who has ever felt trapped by their own negative thoughts, I offer this advice: Challenge your thoughts, reframe your perspective, and take action toward your goals. And remember, with the right mindset and determination, anything is possible.

I can't wait to see what you do!

Euronda Travis, MS, LPC, LSATP

Meet the Author | Euronda Travis, MS, LPC, LSATP

Euronda Travis is a licensed professional counselor, licensed substance abuse practitioner, and a board-approved clinical supervisor for those pursuing licensure in the state of Virginia, boasting over three decades of clinical expertise across diverse settings. She earned her master's degree in rehabilitation counseling from the esteemed Medical College of Virginia at Virginia Commonwealth University in 1997, laying the foundation for her career.

With a rich background encompassing community-based mental health programs, crisis intervention, non-profits, government agencies, and private practice, Euronda's professional journey reflects a steadfast commitment to holistic care. As a licensed professional counselor supervisor, she has mentored and guided countless counseling students, counseling interns, and seasoned professionals, shaping the next generation of mental health practitioners.

Euronda's clinical prowess shines through her adept handling of various challenges faced by children and families, specializing in trauma, separation, loss, adoption-related issues, and depression. Her therapeutic approach is characterized by a seamless integration of evidence-based modalities, including cognitive behavioral therapy, solution focused therapy, dialectical behavior therapy, and mindfulness practices. She is a trauma-informed therapist and believes that everyone has the right to heal.

Central to Euronda's philosophy is a collaborative partnership with clients, empowering them to leverage their innate strengths in overcoming obstacles and achieving personal growth.

In 2016, Euronda founded Comprehensive Counseling Solutions of Virginia in Chesterfield. As the founder and leader of a dedicated team comprising more than thirty mental health professionals, she remains steadfast in her commitment to placing clients' well-being at the forefront. The agency offers a comprehensive array of assessments and treatments, ranging from alcohol and drug assessments, immigration assessments to crisis intervention and intensive in-home services as well as clinic-based intensive outpatient services, catering to individuals and families in need of support.

Beyond her clinical practice, Euronda is deeply engaged in community outreach, forging partnerships with local mental health agencies and private entities to raise awareness about trauma-related issues, particularly within Hispanic and African American communities in the greater Richmond area.

Euronda also heads up Euronda Travis Consulting, an agency that is focused on empowering and coaching high-performing females to overcome mental obstacles to start the life-changing journey from employee to entrepreneur. Her work as an entrepreneur has garnered her many awards and accolades over the last three decades. Most recently, she was named as one of the *Richmond Times Dispatch*'s 2024 Women Who Drive Richmond.

Outside her professional endeavors, Euronda finds fulfillment in her role as a devoted spouse, mother to two accomplished daughters, and a member of Delta Sigma Theta Sorority, Incorporated.

To learn more about Comprehensive Counseling Solutions of Virginia, visit www.myccsva.com and to get more information on Euronda's consulting firm, please visit www.EurondaTravis-Consulting.com

Even as Your Soul Prospers

Ifedayo Greenway

"Ms. Greenway, in my office you don't get to be the coach—only the patient. I'm starting you on medication and taking you out of work for a few weeks. You need time to heal."

I sat across from my doctor sensing the moisture of unmanageable tears running down my face, and to some extent feeling like I had failed myself. I'm a transformational coach and writer, how could I have missed the signs pointing me to my next "change exit"? I encourage and empower women to willingly embrace the pivotal shifts in their lives. Why was I in a place of change by force where I had no options but to comply with my doctor's demands?

It was January 4, 2023. The year had just begun. I was hopeful that 2023 would be better than the year before, and I was ready to prosper—flourish in my life, business, and career. Every year at my church, we start the year off with a new word. The word for 2023 was *positioning*. It had been declared the year of being promoted or arranged in a particular way, which from a business perspective leads to prosperity. Yet, here I was having to pull away from the proverbial line of positioning to heal.

15

Just four months before that doctor's appointment, in September 2022, my family experienced a significant loss. My ex-husband and the father of my daughter had succumbed to his battle with Lou Gehrig's disease (also known as ALS). We knew the day would come because for seven years, we had watched his quality of life deteriorate, but the news of his death still felt like an unimaginable shock. Helping my daughter to deal with the loss of her daddy took every ounce of strength I had. I don't know if there are enough characters on my keyboard for me to type and try to articulate the daddy-daughter bond those two shared. I thought they were inseparable—that is until ALS forced an involuntary departure between them. Supporting her, and sometimes bearing the emotions of my daughter, exceeded my heart's capacity.

Two weeks after he died, I hosted my annual transformation event, The Change Experience. I had thought about canceling it, but I had confidence in my team. I was sure that they were capable of running the event and even facilitating the attendees during the moments when I was emotionally absent, so I went forth with a two-day conference that would require me to physically show up and pour into the lives of the women who had invested money and time in their personal-change experiences.

In October 2022, a few weeks after my event, I launched a new book collaboration project—I know what y'all are thinking, I must have been crazy. Twelve women joined me as their visionary author to write a book that was designed to be a healing journey for the fragments of our broken hearts. I was responsible for coaching and helping them tell their heart stories. So, in a sense, I took on the weight of their broken hearts (with little regard for the shattered pieces of mine) as I coached them through unveiling their narratives.

As November arrived, we embraced a new juncture in our grief journey as we faced the challenge of getting through our first holiday season without my daughter's father. His absence was just as profound as his presence. My daughter had never celebrated a holiday or monumental moment in her life without her daddy. We navigated through the joyful but poignant memories. In December, just two weeks before Christmas, my daughter turned sixteen, and boy, did I throw her the party of her life. Her daddy and I had always planned big birthday celebrations for her, and I wasn't going to let this milestone year be any different.

If I'm honest, organizing it was a blur. I don't even know how I steered through the event-planning moments without crashing, burning, or fizzling completely out. But when the day came, we partied hard, you hear me! We rolled into Christmas on the declining end of our ebbs-and-flows season. Coming down off her birthday celebration, quite naturally she struggled with her first Christmas without her HotShot (that was her superhero nickname for her daddy). We maneuvered through the happiness of her opening her favorite gifts and the sessions of her sobbing as she accepted the fact that she'd never hear him wish her a Merry Christmas again.

I was juggling a lot of things at once. In addition to all those things I just mentioned, I was working a nine-to-five job, actively involved in ministry, and fulfilling contractual obligations with my other book publishing clients.

So, you can imagine that by the time January came on the scene, I was struggling to see the "happy" in the New Year; my gas tank was far below empty, and exhaustion had crept in without asking for my permission. But I certainly didn't want to miss what had been spiritually declared by my pastor as the year of positioning, so I was fully prepared to keep pushing through the grief-stricken fatigue—until that day at my doctor's office.

It was just supposed to be a regular yearly physical. I thought I would knock that appointment off of my to-do list and keep it moving. However, during the appointment, I found myself weeping uncontrollably when my doctor asked me a simple question: "Ms. Greenway, how are you?"

Although I couldn't respond verbally, the deep exhale, excessive tears, and look of hopelessness on my face conveyed my message quite clearly; a deep stare into my eyes revealed my truth. My nonverbal communication was screaming, "I am not okay." The silent cry that erupted from the depths of my soul sent a smoke signal that required immediate attention. I thought I could talk myself out of what I knew my doctor could see. I tried to be my own life coach and said all the things I would say to a client: "I just need to set some different goals," "I am strong enough to endure this," "I can't give up now. I can get through this."

And that's when my doctor gently scolded me. "In my office, you're just the patient, not the coach." It was time to address the overwhelming grief, fatigue, stress, anger, and even depression that I had been sweeping under the rug so that I could continue doing what I assumed was prospering in my everyday life. I agreed and yielded to her plan of reclaiming my wellness.

Days and weeks went by, and I was adjusting to spending most of my time doing very little with my days. My body was also regulating the medication that was supposed to help with my mood. There were days when I would just allow myself to feel whatever I needed to, which resulted in me either crying on the floor or lying in bed for hours. On other days, I would go for a walk or curl up in Barnes and Noble with my favorite coffee drink and read a self-healing or self-help book (*Good Boundaries and Goodbyes* by Lysa TerKeurst changed my entire life). Some days I celebrated the much-needed break, while other days I sulked, feeling like I had lost control of everything. It felt like I had been positioned and was stuck in a fruitless, introspective pit of emotions.

I remember pulling up social media one day and scrolling through my timeline. Looking at the posts of what others were doing in their lives and businesses made me feel sad and unproductive. I was in the slow lane of my entrepreneurial journey, and traffic was zooming past me. It felt like I was being punished—like I had to go off and sit in the corner by myself. I wanted so badly to be in the hustle and bustle of the innovative go-getter grind.

Days later, I was talking to my business coach, and I was complaining about being in such a "still" place in my life and business. I don't remember what she said verbatim, but the essence of her statement was a reminder that sometimes being in a place of healing is the exact position that God wants us to be in. Healing is the productive work that needs to be at the top of the to-do list.

Immediately, my mind drifted to a familiar scripture in the Bible, and I pulled it up to read, *"Beloved, I wish above all things that you may prosper and be in good health even as your soul prospers"* (3 John 1:2 KJV).

Bay-beh! It was the *even as* for me. The compilation of the two words together implies that two things are happening simultaneously. In this context, when the word *even* stands alone, it functions as an adverb and places emphasis on something that is unusual or unexpected. But when used with *as,* it becomes a conjunction linking two or more events together and indicating the equality or sameness of time. Which means I can be a powerhouse and a work in progress at the same time. I am allowed to be imperfect and confident at the same time. Positioning and healing can happen at the same time. Soul nurturing can equal productivity and progression at the same time!

After the passing of my ex-husband, I was overwhelmed with responsibility, some of which was valid and some of which was the false sense of the word. I carried my pain, my daughter's pain, and the pain of my adult sons who acknowledged him as a father figure at some point in their lives. Although our blended family chain was suffering from a broken link, I wanted to keep going. I wanted to be strong for everyone else, keep my entrepreneurial business afloat, stay productive on my day job, and continue to help women write and tell their stories. But the truth is, my narrative had experienced a gut-wrenching plot twist. I was heartsick.

My heartbeat was out of sync with the rhythm of prosperity. My soul was crushed and overtaken by pain. And if you've never experienced it before, soul pain is much different than surface pain. It's the kind of affliction that causes mental, spiritual, social, and sometimes even physical distress. When your soul hurts, *everything hurts,* and life can feel like a redundant chore without meaning. Every day is a challenge. Nothing feels like it will get better, and you get tired of the redundant day-to-day activities. When my doctor considered including medication in my wellness plan, she said, "Ms. Greenway, I know that you are going to get up every day and keep going. My concern is how much effort you have to put into simple things like getting out of the bed in the morning."

My ex-husband was gone and resting in peace, while meanwhile, back at the ranch, I felt like a dead man walking—wrestling with the pieces of grief that his death left behind.

Getting out of bed some days to push myself to be great was definitely a laborious chore. One day, during lunch with an acquaintance, I shared with him that I was kind of on a "forced sabbatical" and gave him the details of some of my emotional challenges. His response was, "Nobody would have ever thought that you didn't have it all together."

I was taken aback by this statement and questioned his motives for saying it. For a moment, it felt like he gained pleasure from knowing what appeared to him as my flaws. And for that reason, he'll never be anything else to me other than an acquaintance. But I also wondered if I had worked too hard to present an unrealistic image of myself to others, pretending that everything was fine when I was in emotional fragments. Perhaps I had convinced myself that I was okay even when I wasn't. My doctor was right! It was time to do something different. I needed to pivot, shift in my process, and reprioritize things. This realization was profound because it shifted my perspective. Instead of viewing my current stillness as a setback, I began to see it as a season of preparation and strategic positioning.

I wanted to focus on prospering in ways that I thought would be the most beneficial for me—making money and growing my business—but God (through the words of my business coach) was reminding me that soul prosperity was a priority. There are times when completely focusing on healing is necessary, but there are also moments where healing can happen *even as* other things in my life are happening. I could not afford to miss the command to surrender to simultaneous commitments. If I failed to focus on the "same timeness" of my wellness journey, I risked missing out on stand-alone blessings that would rain on a heart that had been cultivated for healing.

Just like a seed planted in the ground, there is a period where it seems like nothing is happening. But beneath the surface, roots are spreading, and growth is taking place. In the same way, God was working in me, preparing me to be positioned for greater by rehabilitating my soul.

I started to embrace this time of healing and restoration, knowing that it was a crucial part of my journey toward wholeness. I realized that true prosperity encompasses more than just external markers of success. It's about the internal richness of the soul, the depth of our relationships, and the resilience of our spirits. It's about finding meaning and purpose even in the midst of recovering from pain and loss.

A few transformation lessons that I learned along the way:

1. **Understand the power of vulnerability.** True healing often begins with vulnerability; the state of being emotionally exposed. Allow yourself to acknowledge and express your emotions without judgment. This openness

can lead to deeper self-understanding and acceptance, fostering a sense of peace and growth. When we're vulnerable, we invite authentic connections with others, creating space for empathy and understanding in our relationships. It was really hard for me to share that I was on "mood medication" because it makes me susceptible to judgment. But I also know that divulging the personal details tears down the stigma associated with the private shame.

2. **Seize the season of stillness.** Just as a seed needs time under ground to grow roots before sprouting, embrace stillness as a season of preparation and growth. Allow yourself the time and space to heal and restore, nurturing your soul with practices that are conducive to raising the needle on your progress meter. For me, it was prayer, reading, devotions, and journaling. Stillness allows us to listen to our inner voice, gaining clarity and insight that may be drowned out by the noise of our busy lives.

3. **Embrace your "even as" season.** Life often presents us with situations where seemingly conflicting elements coexist. Embracing the "even as" season teaches us to find balance and harmony in the midst of life's contradictions, understanding that growth often occurs in the tension between opposing forces; two (or more) opposite things can actually be working together for your good. This season invites us to navigate complexity with grace, acknowledging that life's richness often lies in its diversity of experiences and perspective.

Perhaps, one of the most profound lessons I learned during this time was the importance of self-care and self-compassion. I had always been someone who put others' needs before my own, but I came to understand that I couldn't pour from an empty cup. Taking the time to care for myself—mind, body, and soul—was not selfish; it was necessary for my well-being and to promote continued resilience. Through it all, I held on to hope—the belief that better days were ahead, that this season of darkness would eventually give way to a season of light. I found ways to rehydrate my hope even when it was drying up. And slowly but surely, I began to see glimpses of that light shining through. I allowed myself to feel moments of joy and gratitude *even as* my heart was full of sorrow, moments that reminded me that life can be beautiful and broken at the same time.

As I continue on this journey of healing and restoration, I carry with me the lessons I've learned and the wisdom I've gained. I know that there will be challenges ahead, but I also know that I am stronger and more resilient than I ever thought possible. God has begun the process of removing the fragments of my broken heart story, and I am grateful for every step of this journey. It has been the beacon of light leading me to a place of deeper understanding, deeper compassion, and deeper peace. Writing this chapter made me curious about how different versions of the Bible would interpret the same scripture that I shared earlier (3 John 1:2), so I looked it up. The additional variations brought even more comfort to my soul.

The Message version says, "*...and I pray for good fortune in everything you do, and for your good health—that your everyday affairs prosper, as well as your soul.*" While the Amplified version puts it this way, "*Beloved, I pray that in every way you may succeed and prosper and be in good health [physically] just as I know your soul prospers [spiritually].*" I journeyed over to the New International Version, and it read, "*Dear friend, I pray that you may enjoy good health and that all may go well with you, even as your soul is getting along.*"

Each translation offers a slightly different angle, yet all convey the underlying message of well-being and prosperity, both physical and spiritual. They aligned me with the realization of the interconnectedness between different aspects of my life, and how focusing on soul prosperity can lead to overall flourishing.

I truly believe that in addition to her professional responsibility, my doctor was conveying the same message that I'll leave you with:

Dear friend, I pray that you may enjoy a wholesome life and that all may go well with you, even as your soul is getting along. May you find the courage to face your pain, the strength to heal, and the faith to believe that brighter days are ahead. May you succeed, do well financially, flourish, thrive, and be in good health, *even as your soul prospers.*

Meet the Author | Ifedayo Greenway

Ifedayo Greenway is a mother, speaker, and master life coach.

She is the chief executive officer of IG & MORE LLC. As a transformational coach, Ifedayo produces an annual event, The Change Experience, which empowers women to embrace the power of change in their lives.

She is the founder of the She Unveils movement where she serves and helps others accomplish their literary goals through unveiling, writing, and publishing their stories. She has been featured in *Huffington Post,* CBS, FOX, NBC, and *Shoutout Atlanta* for her literary works (*Removing The Face* and *Removing The Fear*).

Ifedayo is a prolific author who has written seven books, four of which have been bestsellers. She holds the position of visionary author in three of those publications. Along with these books, she has also written inspirational articles that have reached thousands of readers through various mediums such as *Thrive Global* and *Faith Heart Magazine.*

Ifedayo is passionate about her covenant with God to impact the world and uses her journey to strengthen and encourage women to find their authentic voice in their pursuit of transformation.

Connect with her at www.igandmore.com.

The Overnight Success and the Self-Made Millionaire

A Fairy Tale
Maya Lynn Harris

One of my favorite singers is Toni Braxton. Her sultry voice, her style, her haircut—I loved and still love everything about her. Of course, we know about her and her sisters, but a lot of people don't know how she was discovered. The story is that Toni was at a gas station in Atlanta one day, standing at her car pumping gas and a talent scout just happened to be inside the gas station. Toni was singing along with the music that was playing over the loudspeaker, and the scout was blown away by her voice. He invited her to meet a producer, and the rest, as they say, is history. She was an overnight success.

Madam CJ Walker is documented as the first female self-made millionaire. She was a giant in the hair care industry and helped thousands of women become entrepreneurs in their own right. Due to her own hair issues like severe dandruff and alopecia, she looked for ways to solve the hair care problems that many African-American women experienced. She developed her own line of hair care products and deployed a unique marketing team (practically an army) of twenty thousand saleswomen by 1917 who sold her hair care products across the country.

I've always been inspired by Toni's discovery and Madam CJ Walker's vision. But both stories contain a major flaw. They're both based on myths.

Toni had actually been working for years and years as a singer, singing background in churches, choirs, and small clubs before she got her big break at this gas station. She did not plan to be discovered that day, but she had already put in the work so that when the opportunity presented itself, she was ready. Nothing happened "overnight" for Toni.

Madam CJ Walker learned her earliest lessons in hair care from her brothers who were barbers. She also then spent many years under the tutelage of Annie Malone, a hair care industry giant in her own right, as a saleswoman for Malone's Poro product line. Malone even accused Walker of stealing her formula, making minor adjustments, and then selling it as her own. While Madam CJ Walker experienced incredible success, she certainly was not "self-made."

We live in a microwave society. Everyone wants everything to happen right now. We want our food to be fast, our information to be instant, and our weight loss to happen with a pill or a shot. Sometimes it seems folks don't want to work anymore. Everyone wants to be "Insta-famous." But I have learned that with any person's success story that seemed to happen instantaneously, there are two truths: 1) It did not happen overnight and 2) They did not do it alone. Real success, real prosperity still happens the same way it has always happened—with prayer, a lot of support, and a whole lot of effort.

Now, don't get me wrong. Technology has helped us quite a bit to make our processes happen faster and more efficiently. But that does not mean you don't have to work at it. Working smarter simply means you understand that you no longer have to deal with everything alone. The support is out there, and it can actually help you in your efforts.

Let me not pretend that I have done everything right as I preach from the soapbox. When I started my organization W.O.M.B. (Woman-Owned Minority Businesses), it came from the need to figure out what to do with my office space once I had decided to walk away from my tutoring company. I owned LAMA Learning for five years and finally decided to close it once my parents moved to Virginia. It was just too much to run the business and take care of them at the same time. But I had four office suites and about nine months left on the lease. What was I going to do? I did not plan for an exit from my business. No, I didn't even know that I should plan for an exit, or I would have handled it much better. After all, I had already helped quite a few people get their businesses started. You would think I understood the entire cycle of the business, but here I was, walking away from one company, trying to figure out how to fill the space so that I wouldn't completely go bankrupt in the process.

I had a networking group called SHE for a couple of years. We would meet once a month at a local coffee shop where we would share ideas, listen to our guest speakers, and introduce our businesses to each other. The event had about twenty women who would attend regularly and had seen well over one hundred women during the course of its lifetime. SHE wasn't intended to be a full-time business; it was just a way for me to connect with other women and create space for women entrepreneurs who were basically ignored by existing networking groups. But I loved the idea of what we had created and put it on the backburner while I focused on securing an admin position at a school.

Fast forward to 2019. The tutoring company I had started after leaving my twenty-five-plus-year career as a teacher was also now coming to an end. I had no idea what my next step was going to be, but I knew I had to think quickly. How in the world could I use this space? I thought about the clients I had for business planning. Maybe I could teach more classes. That would at least generate enough income to break even and pay for the space. What else could I do to pay for the space, bring people together, and replace what I was losing with LAMA? Then I remembered SHE. I remembered how great it felt to be in a room filled with other women entrepreneurs. I remembered how much we learned from each other and how much my business had grown as a result. So, I considered relaunching the monthly event at the space. But then I looked around and realized that there was a lot more potential in this space than just a monthly event. We could actually come together and do more events, or even use it as a co-op space. That made a lot of sense! I was ready to jump in and get started. But then I remembered that my lack of planning had led me to where I was at that moment: an entrepreneur with no business and way too many bills. If I was going to be successful this time around, I had to plan, I had to prepare, and I had to humble myself enough to get help.

I started with a plan. Instead of simply going to Google and downloading a template, I decided to get professional help. Even as someone who helps other people create business plans for a living, I knew it was important to solicit the help and support from others with more experience and an unbiased eye. I started by attending a SCORE workshop. If you're not familiar with SCORE, it is a nonprofit leg of the Small Business Administration that connects new business owners to resources, training, and mentors. The SCORE workshop quickly revealed the holes in my plan for W.O.M.B. Believe it or not, I was excited at these discoveries because it allowed me to fix issues before they happened. So, I created my business plan using an alternative method called the business model canvas. It's a tool that many businesses use for initial startup and ongoing business planning. Using this tool was a solid start, but I knew additional input would be needed.

I reached out to a friend of mine who was and is an exceptional business coach. Doctor Shantelle Chambliss is the founder of Nonprofitability, and she specifically works with nonprofit founders. But I also knew that she had a solid business model, would not bite her tongue with the advice that she would give, and had my best interests at heart, so I scheduled a strategy session with her. She took a look at my original business plan, my business model canvas, and other ideas that I had written down in various notebooks, and within a couple of hours, we had a solid foundation for W.O.M.B. It probably was one of the most painful experiences I had ever gone through as a business owner! Sis did *not* hold back! But this is the power of partnering with a coach who genuinely wants to see you succeed. Not to mention, working with a sister who not only was your critic but also your cheerleader.

Once I had a solid plan in place, I put together my launch plan. Trust me, it was counterintuitive because I really just wanted to create a website and put it out there for the world to see and sit back and wait for the thousands of women to join.

Don't laugh at me, sis. I know better now!

I created a series of small networking sessions and invited women who had attended my SHE events. During those sessions, I got feedback on what the attendees were looking for when it came to networking and growing their businesses. Then based on their input, I developed a membership for the new organization. I reached back out to those ladies and invited them into our pre-launch. We started with twenty-five members, all women entrepreneurs with whom I had already built relationships who trusted me enough to join me on this new journey.

I then began to reach out to business coaches and industry experts whom I had connected with over the years to host trainings on the topics that the networking session attendees had mentioned in their surveys. Not only did we now have solid training from vetted professionals, but the coaches now had an additional network to prospect clients of their own from! Those relationships—even ones I had cultivated five to ten years ago—proved to be vital to the launch of my business. Imagine if my only focus was to make the next sale and get the next client rather than making relationship building a priority. Those relationships were and continue to be the cornerstone of W.O.M.B.

When COVID hit and the world went inside, just like every other entrepreneur, I had to figure out how to keep my business going. It was going to require I pivot into the virtual space. You know what that meant? It meant I had to adjust my plan! Everyone was running to the internet to keep their business afloat. New tools were popping up every day, along with new opportunities. I knew I did not have an enormous amount of time to work out the perfect plan, but I knew I had to be thoughtful and deliberate. I changed the structure of the networking sessions and created chapters. Initially, the chapters were based on where you were in your business. We had chapters for our pre-planners, our launchers, our builders, and our expanders. And would you believe I thought that I was going to be able to run each chapter?

Wait. Are you laughing again?

I quickly realized that I was burning the candle at both ends and in the middle. Something had to be done. So, I created a new type of strategic partnership, the circle leader. The circle leader would be in charge of each circle (aka chapter) in exchange for a free membership. This allowed me to continue to focus on the business of running the business.

Due to the success of our circle leaders, we survived the pandemic. We didn't come out unscathed, but we survived. Today, W.O.M.B. continues to grow with members from nineteen states with eight circles/chapters, and more than twenty volunteer leaders. We've been blessed and continue to focus on our goal of supporting black and brown women entrepreneurs all around the world.

In my journey as an entrepreneur, I've walked paths riddled with uncertainties, faced challenges head-on, and embraced opportunities with passion. Through it all, I've come to appreciate the transformative power of planning and partnerships. From that power, three foundational principles have guided me toward prosperity, embodying the essence of my entrepreneurial spirit.

Plan for the Person You Want to Be, Not the Person You Are

As I embarked on my entrepreneurial journey, I realized that success isn't just about where you are—it's about where you're heading. It's about having a clear vision of the person you aspire to become and laying down the groundwork to reach that destination. This principle has been the cornerstone of my journey, guiding my actions, decisions, and aspirations.

Planning for the person you want to be requires a blend of foresight, ambition, and strategic thinking. It's about transcending your current circumstances and envisioning a future filled with possibilities. For me, this meant setting big, hairy, audacious goals, challenging my limits, and daring to dream big.

One of the most pivotal moments in my entrepreneurial journey was when I made a conscious decision to envision my future self—the successful, empowered entrepreneur I aspired to become. I mapped out my goals, visualized my trajectory, and crafted a roadmap to turn my vision into reality. This shift in mindset propelled me forward, empowering me to overcome obstacles, seize opportunities, and navigate the complexities of entrepreneurship with clarity and purpose.

But planning for the person you want to be isn't just about setting lofty goals; it's also about taking concrete steps to turn your vision into reality. This may involve acquiring new skills, expanding your network, or pursuing opportunities that align with your long-term aspirations. For me, it meant investing in professional development, seeking mentorship from seasoned entrepreneurs, and surrounding myself with like-minded peers who shared my vision and ambition.

As I reflect on this principle, I'm reminded of the countless times it has guided me through moments of doubt and uncertainty. Whether it was launching a new venture, pivoting in the face of adversity, or charting a new course toward uncharted territories, planning for the person I wanted to be gave me the clarity, confidence, and conviction to pursue my dreams with unwavering determination.

Surround Yourself with Forward-Thinking People

Success is rarely achieved in isolation. It thrives in an ecosystem of support, collaboration, and shared vision. That's why I've always emphasized the importance of surrounding yourself with forward-thinking individuals who inspire, challenge, and uplift you on your entrepreneurial journey.

From the early days of my career to the present moment, I've been fortunate to have crossed paths with remarkable individuals who have left an indelible mark on my journey. Whether it was mentors who offered invaluable guidance, peers who provided unwavering support, or advisors who challenged me to think differently, each person played a crucial role in shaping my entrepreneurial path.

Building a network of like-minded peers, mentors, and advisors isn't just about finding individuals who share your vision—it's also about cultivating a culture of innovation and collaboration within your own community. It's about creating spaces where ideas are celebrated, perspectives are valued, and diverse voices are heard.

One of the most profound experiences I've had in my entrepreneurial journey was when I founded W.O.M.B. Our monthly gatherings have become a space for collaboration, inspiration, and empowerment, where women from diverse backgrounds come together to share ideas, support each other's ventures, and celebrate each other's successes. The energy and enthusiasm that fills the room during those gatherings are palpable, reminding me of the transformative power of community and collaboration.

But surrounding yourself with forward-thinking people isn't just about building a network—it's also about fostering meaningful connections and nurturing relationships that extend beyond the confines of business. It's about finding mentors who believe in your potential, peers who challenge you to grow, and advisors who offer sage advice and guidance.

As I look back on my journey, I'm grateful for the countless individuals who have supported me, challenged me, and inspired me to reach new heights of success. Their wisdom, guidance, and encouragement have been invaluable assets on my entrepreneurial journey, empowering me to overcome obstacles, seize opportunities, and navigate the complexities of entrepreneurship with confidence and resilience.

A Written Plan Is Your Map to Prosperity

In the whirlwind of entrepreneurship, it's easy to get swept up in the chaos of day-to-day operations and lose sight of the bigger picture. That's where a written plan comes in. It serves as your roadmap, guiding your actions, priorities, and decisions toward your ultimate goals.

A written plan forces you to clarify your vision, articulate your objectives, and map out the steps needed to achieve them. It provides a tangible framework for tracking progress, measuring success, and holding yourself accountable along the way.

But a written plan is more than just a static document—it's a living, breathing blueprint for your entrepreneurial journey. It should be revisited, revised, and refined regularly to reflect changing circumstances, new insights, and evolving goals. By keeping your plan dynamic and adaptive, you can stay agile in the face of uncertainty and navigate toward prosperity with confidence and clarity.

The path to prosperity is paved with intention, vision, and strategic planning. By planning for the person you want to be, surrounding yourself with forward-thinking people, and committing your vision to paper, you can chart a course toward success that is as empowering as it is enduring. As you embark on your own journey, remember, the power to prosper lies within you waiting to be unleashed.

Meet the Author | Maya Lynn Harris

After years of running her own ventures, Maya Lynn Harris realized that her greatest passion was to help women monetize their skills and talents. As a strategic planning coach, Maya teaches women how to plan, implement, and execute a sustainable, purposeful business. However, she also recognized the need for entrepreneurs like herself to have a safe space to grow their businesses as a community. So, she founded W.O.M.B. (Woman-Owned Minority Business), a professional organization committed to training black/brown women entrepreneurs to increase their profits through strategic planning, partnerships, and promotions.

She is the author of *What's Your Oil? Unmasking Your Hidden Talents,* a book about her journey into entrepreneurship and its parallel to the Biblical story of the widow's oil of II Kings, Chapter 4.

Maya, a Connecticut native, received her B.A. in English from Virginia Union University and her M.S. in educational leadership from Walden University. She taught secondary English in Connecticut and Virginia for more than twenty-five years and finished her career in education as a secondary English instructional coach. She has two wonderful sons, Mandell and Bryce, and now resides in Richmond, Virginia.

. . .

Connect with Maya at:

W.O.M.B.: https://wombbiz.org

Maya Harris: https://mayalynnharris.com

Email: maya@wombbiz.org

Calendar: https://callmaya.com

How to Prosper
Step One
Jean Tillery

rosper. A verb that means to thrive, succeed, or flourish in various aspects of life, such as financially, socially, emotionally, or intellectually

When someone prospers, they experience growth, advancement, and positive outcomes in their endeavors. This could mean achieving financial stability, realizing personal goals, building strong relationships, making meaningful contributions to society, or experiencing overall well-being and fulfillment.

Prosperity is often associated with abundance, progress, and the attainment of desired outcomes, reflecting a state of flourishing, and thriving in one's life circumstances.

We all have a feeling of what "prosper" means, but do we know what "prosper" looks like? You see, that is the difficulty with defining prosperity. It looks like something different to each of us.

My name is Jean Tillery, and my company is Epic Living with Jean. I offer products, programs, connections, and community to help you discover, build, and live a life that you would call #epic. That is the key—what *you* would call epic. Epic is different for every person, and it could be different every day. Even every hour.

I am a certified dream manager. What that means is that I help my clients identify and then fulfill their dreams. The first step in this process is identification. It is the same first step that must happen when you are considering prosperity. You need to identify what that definition is to you.

I want to take this time to guide you through the first step of building prosperity by helping you identify your unique definition.

The Essence of Prosperity

As a dream manager, I have twelve areas of our lives that we build dreams for. These areas can be used in your consideration of prosperity also. Here are just a few: physical, emotional, financial, creative, and legacy.

Throughout history, there has been more emphasis on some areas than others. Think about it: The cavemen were much more concerned about survival, so physical prosperity would be high on their list.

Your nationality, culture, or religion may play a role in the definition of prosperity. Take the country of Bhutan for example. Their approach to prosperity has led to policies that protect the environment, promote cultural heritage, and ensure that development is sustainable and benefits the population's well-being. They have inspired discussions worldwide about the importance of measuring prosperity, not just by economic output, but by the happiness and well-being of the people.

Compare that to the United States. Our gross domestic product numbers measure the total dollar value of all goods and services produced over a specific time within the country's borders and is widely used to gauge the economic performance of the country. It is frequently interpreted as a proxy for the standard of living and by extension, the level of prosperity within the country.

The Diversity of Prosperity

Prosperity is not a one-size-fits-all concept. It is experienced, understood, and valued differently. This diversity stems from several factors that influence how prosperity is perceived and defined. Understanding these factors can help individuals and communities better articulate their unique visions of prosperity and work toward achieving them.

Personal Values and Beliefs

One's personal values and beliefs fundamentally shape what one considers to be a prosperous life. For some, prosperity might be primarily defined in financial terms—achieving wealth and material success. For others, it might mean living a life aligned with their values, such as having a fulfilling career, contributing to their community, or maintaining close relationships. These intrinsic values guide individuals' priorities and decisions, influencing their definition of prosperity.

Cultural and Social Influences

Cultural backgrounds and societal norms play a significant role in shaping definitions of prosperity. Different cultures prioritize various aspects of life, from communal harmony and family bonds to individual achievement and innovation. Societal expectations can also pressure individuals to conform to a certain standard of success, such as achieving a high level of education, owning property, or attaining a prestigious career.

. . .

Economic Environment

The economic context in which a person lives affects their perception of prosperity. In regions where basic needs are a daily concern, financial stability and security might be the primary indicators of prosperity. In more affluent societies, the focus may shift toward personal fulfillment, self-actualization, and quality of life beyond mere financial success.

Life Experiences

Individual life experiences, including successes, failures, and everything in between, significantly influence one's definition of prosperity. These experiences shape an individual's worldview, resilience, and aspirations. For example, someone who has overcome significant challenges may prioritize emotional well-being and resilience as key components of their prosperity.

Age and Life Stage

People's definitions of prosperity often evolve as they move through different stages of life. Young adults might equate prosperity with career success and exploration, while older adults may place more value on health, relationships, and legacy. Each life stage brings different priorities and challenges, influencing how prosperity is defined and pursued.

Personal Goals and Aspirations

Individual goals and dreams also affect the definition of prosperity. Someone with a passion for travel might define prosperity as the freedom and means to explore the world, while another person might aim for a prosperous life through creative expression or innovation in their field.

Global and Technological Changes

The rapid pace of technological advancement and global interconnectedness has also redefined prosperity. Access to information, digital connectivity, and new economic opportunities can shift perceptions of what it means to live a prosperous life, emphasizing adaptability, lifelong learning, and digital literacy as new dimensions of success.

Given these diverse influences, prosperity cannot be universally defined. Rather, it is a deeply personal concept that reflects a combination of individual aspirations, cultural backgrounds, societal pressures, and life circumstances. Recognizing and respecting this diversity is crucial for individuals and societies aiming to foster true prosperity for all.

Identifying What *Your* Prosperity Means

That leads us to how you identify what the definition of prosperity is to you.

I have what I call "Dream Storms" for my clients, where I have a series of questions that I ask them that lead them into the process, and these same questions can be used here.

What does your ideal day look like? This encourages you to envision a life where you feel prosperous and gives you a chance to identify the elements that contribute to your happiness and fulfillment. Where do you live? What type of house? When do you wake up? Do you work? Do you volunteer? What do you eat? How and where? Do you have family that lives with you? Do you have children?

What are your core values? Core values are defined as the fundamental beliefs and guiding principles that dictate behaviors and actions and serve as a compass. They influence your decisions, shape your goals, and they serve as a framework for your definition of prosperity. For example, if one of my core values is to always have my young children as my top priority, the ability to travel may not be a sign of prosperity for me, but being able to send my children to college might be. I encourage everyone I work with to have a set of values for themselves personally, for their family, and for their business if they have one. It is important to align your life with your fundamental beliefs for genuine prosperity.

How do you define success in your five pillars? Have you heard of the work/life balance? I do not think that is an accurate picture of life, especially for women. I teach instead that there are five pillars in our lives—mind, body, soul, relationships, and work. There will never be a true balance of each one—life is always an ebb and flow—but for me, prosperity means having employment that allows me to save Sunday for worship and to take the holidays off to enjoy my family. That is why I have my own business.

What does financial freedom mean to you? It should go beyond wealth accumulation and include security, the ability to pursue your passions, or the freedom to give generously. For many years, prosperity for me meant being able to pay my bills when I got them and not having to save up to pay them. After I reached that point, prosperity meant having a savings account with money to cover unexpected problems as they popped up.

How do you want to impact the world? Think about your legacy. There are broader implications of your prosperity that can include making a difference in the lives of others—in your family, in your community, and across the world.

These are just a few things to consider as you start to define what prosperity looks like to you.

Barriers to Identifying Prosperity

It can be a struggle to identify *your* version of prosperity due to the barriers that may hinder you from fully understanding or articulating what it means to you.

Here are five common obstacles and a way to overcome them.

1. Societal pressure and family, or generational ideas of prosperity. Social media can lead us to a warped idea of what prosperity means. The constant bombardment of societal standards and the tendency to compare oneself with others can color our personal values and aspirations, making it difficult to identify what truly constitutes prosperity on an individual level.

Overcoming Strategy: Cultivate self-awareness and gratitude for your own journey. Practice mindfulness and focus on your own goals and achievements instead of comparing yourself to others. Keeping a gratitude journal can help shift focus from what you lack to what you have achieved and possess.

Dedicate time regularly for self-reflection. Use journaling, meditation, or walks in nature to contemplate your true desires, values, and what prosperity means to you. This practice can provide clarity and help you understand your unique path.

2. Fear of change or failure. Fear can be a significant barrier to defining and pursuing personal prosperity. The apprehension about leaving comfort zones, risking failure, or facing the unknown can prevent individuals from exploring or acknowledging their true aspirations.

Overcoming Strategy: Embrace a growth mindset. View failures and challenges as opportunities to learn and grow. Start with small, manageable risks to build confidence, and gradually challenge yourself more as your comfort zone expands.

3. Undefined goals or visions. A lack of clear, articulated goals or visions for one's life can make it challenging to identify a path to prosperity. Ambiguity in what one aims to achieve leads to difficulty in measuring progress and fulfillment. If we are not clear on our vision, it is extremely easy to adapt other people's vision as our own.

Overcoming Strategy: Set clear, specific, and achievable goals. Break down your vision of prosperity into tangible steps and objectives. Use visualization techniques to keep your goals vivid in your mind, reinforcing your commitment and direction.

4. Overemphasis on material wealth. While financial stability is an aspect of prosperity, an overemphasis on material wealth can overshadow other dimensions such as emotional well-being, relationships, and personal growth, leading to a skewed perception of what it means to be prosperous.

Overcoming Strategy: Expand your definition of wealth to include non-material aspects of life, such as relationships, health, and personal growth. Regularly assess and realign your goals to ensure they encompass a holistic view of prosperity.

5. Limited beliefs in possibilities. Self-imposed limitations or a fixed mindset can restrict one's ability to envision a prosperous life beyond current circumstances or past experiences, hindering the identification of a broader, more fulfilling definition of success.

Overcoming Strategy: Challenge limiting beliefs by exposing yourself to new ideas and perspectives. Seek out stories of individuals who have achieved their dreams against the odds. Consider working with a coach or mentor who can help you see beyond your perceived limitations.

I hope these not only provide you with a deeper understanding of the challenges you may face, but also equip you with the insight to navigate these obstacles as you define and pursue your own versions of prosperity.

Actionable Steps Toward Your Prosperity

Here is a list of steps to take as you begin your journey. These steps are created to be practical and impactful and help you to start your journey toward a more prosperous and fulfilling life:

1. **Reflect and Journal.** Start a prosperity journal where you can explore your thoughts and feelings about what prosperity means to you. Reflect on the questions provided above and write down your fears, aspirations, and the barriers you feel are in your way. This practice fosters self-awareness and clarity and allows your brain to begin to see the prosperity potential. It is also useful to go back and look at it when your views are challenged by others, or when you need some encouragement and inspiration to keep working toward prosperity.

2. **Define Your Prosperity Vision.** Create a clear and detailed vision of your prosperous life. This could involve writing a vision statement or creating a vision board that includes all aspects of your life such as career, finances, relationships, health, and personal growth—whichever areas are important to you. The key is specificity and personal significance. This belongs to *you* and no one else.

3. **Set SMART Goals**. Make sure your goals are *specific, measurable, achievable, relevant,* and *time-bound* (SMART)

goals that align with the vision of prosperity. This is more difficult than it sounds. Take the time to get laser focused on what the goals are. Clear, well-defined goals are more actionable and achievable. You need to specify exactly what you want to achieve, why it is important to you, and how you plan to get there. Make sure the goals are realistic based on your current situation.

The next thing to do is to break down these goals into actionable steps. Large goals can feel overwhelming. Break them into smaller tasks that can be accomplished in a reasonable timeframe. This will help you maintain momentum and provide a sense of accomplishment as you progress.

Remember, these goals are not set in stone. Life changes, and so might your aspirations or the means to achieve them. Regularly review your goals to reflect on progress, learn from your setbacks, and adjust your plan, as necessary. Flexibility is crucial to your success. Things might change as you get closer to your version of prosperity.

4. **Cultivate a Support Network.** A support network will provide encouragement, advice, and accountability. Whether it is a professional network, a hobby group, or a social cause, find people with shared interests, goals, and values that align with your vision of prosperity. Take advantage of both online platforms and in-person gatherings.

If you cannot find a tribe that meets your needs, then consider creating one. This can be easier than you think. There are others out there looking for the same things that you are.

Another possibility is to find a mentor or mastermind group. As you are reflecting on your goals, which areas do you need guidance in? Is it expertise in a specific field, career advice, or personal development? Knowing what you need helps in finding a mentor who can truly contribute to your growth. When approaching potential mentors, be clear about why you are seeking their mentorship and what you hope to achieve. Respect their time and contributions by being prepared and proactive in your interactions. A good mentor-mentee relationship is built on mutual respect and clear communication.

5. **Embrace Learning and Growth.** Adopt a mindset that is focused on continuous learning and growth. Seek out resources, courses, workshops, or books that will expand your knowledge and skills in areas related to their prosperity goals. Remember, setbacks are part of the learning process, an opportunity for growth, and sometimes a cue for realignment.

These steps are designed to empower you to take control of your journey toward prosperity and provide you with a structured path to follow. Revisit and adjust your goals and strategies as they evolve, and always remember, the pursuit of prosperity is a dynamic and ongoing process.

The Role of a Dream Manager in Prosperity

I spent eleven years following an "unofficial" version of the dream manager protocol. I was continually amazed at how different your life looks when you clearly define what is important to you.

My role as a dream manager is to guide individuals toward defining and achieving their personal and professional dreams. These dreams are intrinsically linked to their concepts of prosperity. By facilitating this, I become a catalyst for individuals to explore and define what prosperity truly means to them—beyond conventional metrics of success such as wealth and status.

I provide the tools, support, and encouragement necessary for individuals to delve deep into their values, passions, and goals, thereby uncovering a more personalized and fulfilling notion of prosperity. This process not only aids in setting a clear direction for their aspirations but also aligns their daily actions and decisions with their ultimate vision of a prosperous life. My role as a dream manager is not just about helping individuals dream bigger, but also about ensuring that these dreams are in harmony with their core values and that they contribute to a sense of purpose and well-being, reflecting the nature of prosperity itself.

As a dream manager, I am instrumental in transforming the abstract concept of prosperity into a tangible and achievable reality for those I guide, marking a profound comparison to the broader, often impersonal, metrics of prosperity.

Conclusion

Now, I invite you to take the first step on your journey toward personal prosperity. Begin by reflecting on what prosperity truly means to you. What are your core values? What dreams and goals light up your path to fulfillment? It may seem like an overwhelming assignment, but I promise you the time you spend will repay you tenfold as you start to envision your life through the lens of what is important to you. Then you will see how much easier it is to live a life where you are fulfilled and prosperous, by *your* definition. If you need help with this process or are overwhelmed, reach out to me at Epic Living with Jean.

If you are ready to take the next step, ask me how the dream manager program can support you in not just identifying your aspirations but in making them a tangible reality.

Together, let us redefine prosperity, moving beyond traditional metrics to embrace a richer, more diverse, and personally meaningful interpretation. Your epic life awaits—let us dream, plan, and prosper together.

Meet the Author | Jean Tillery

Jean Tillery is a visionary leader and the driving force behind Epic Living with Jean, a pioneering platform dedicated to empowering individuals to lead their most fulfilling lives. As a certified dream manager, Jean combines her expertise in dream realization with her roles as the engaging host of the #epicStories podcast and a passionate ambassador for the Epicure food company, to inspire a community of dreamers and doers.

With a rich background as a home-schooling mom, Jean has honed her skills in teaching, coaching, leadership, creation, and community building. Her journey is a testament to the transformative power of dreams. After years of envisioning a cross-country road trip and overcoming significant physical and mental challenges, including a battle with long COVID, Jean embarked on the #epicRoadtrip. This journey was not only a milestone in her personal dream list but also a mission to share her powerful message on the importance of dreaming with a wider audience.

Follow her on her Facebook page, Epic Living with Jean, and check out her website, www.epiclivingwithjean.com. She would love to talk to you about what #epic looks like to you. Send her an email her at jean@epiclivingwithjean.com.

I Woke Up Like This
Yolanda W. Hall, BS, MEd, CLC

At age twenty-eight, I remember feeling really accomplished. I had earned my bachelor's degree, my master's degree, I'd pledged my life to the best sorority on the planet, and I had just landed my first big-girl job as a school counselor in Henrico County Public Schools. I was rolling around town in my Nissan Altima, and plans were in the works to purchase my first home. Everyone was proud that I was heading in the right direction. I was prospering...I was flourishing...I was growing. But something was missing. It wasn't the fact that I was almost thirty and did not have a ring on my finger. It wasn't that my clock was ticking, as the elders would say, and there were no babies anywhere in sight. I could not put my finger on it, and then one day I had a dream.

I had gotten a call from my father asking me to visit him. It was collect because he was in prison. I remember arriving at the location somewhere in Queens, New York, not far from where I grew up. I walked down the stairs and through a door to a long hallway. After checking in, they took me to a room where there was a chair, a phone, and a glass window like you see in the movies. I sat down, picked up the phone, looked up, and saw my father who was looking at me from the other side of the glass. He had a big smile on his face and a big afro that kinda leaned forward toward his face. There he was looking like 1973! I was getting *Cooley High* vibes, for sure. He looked exactly like he did in the pictures I had seen of him. He picked up the phone on the wall and began talking. I could see his lips moving, but I couldn't hear his voice. I tried desperately to hear him, and the next thing I remember was waking up as if I had the worst nightmare. I was breathing heavily and sitting in the bed holding my forehead thinking, *What in the world? There is no way this could be true!*

It was all a dream.... It was only a dream.

It was a good while before I got the nerve to say anything, then one day while talking to my mother on the phone, I decided to tell her about my dream. As I shared, in a questioning tone, I guess I insinuated there was a possibility they only told me he died when I was two months old because they didn't want me to know that he was locked up. She kinda chuckled and said, "No... He's really dead."

You see, I couldn't hear my father's voice in my dream because I'd never heard his voice in real life.

I have come in order that you might have life—life in all its fullness.

— John 10:10 GNT

I had my first awakening when I came into this world on a Tuesday morning in April. My mother and father were barely in their twenties —a newly married couple with a new baby girl. I'm guessing there was lots of excitement, but amid all the celebrating, who knew our lives would soon be changed forever? In June of that same year, my grandmother got a call at work. Her son—my father—was found unconscious at his job. A combination of emotional trauma and a bad coping strategy took his life. He was gone. I never knew him, and I never heard his voice. All I had was a few random stories and constant references of how much I resembled him.

Wait a minute...that was it! He was what was missing! It was at this point in my life that I became aware that I missed not knowing my father—not having a father, not experiencing my role as his daughter, not having the daddy-daughter connection I'd heard my friends talk about! Was this why I hadn't found "the one," the one my daddy was supposed to prepare me for? Was this why my biological clock was still ticking loudly like an antique grandfather clock in the corner of the room?

As my thirtieth birthday was quickly approaching, I decided to find a therapist. I just needed a place to dump everything that was taking up so much space in my mind. During my time in therapy, I admitted that I was mad at my father for the choices he made instead of choosing me. Little by little, I began to feel a release and eventually was able to forgive him.

Only God knew when He would call my father home. And in my search for answers, He helped me see that my father's life on earth was largely purposed so that I may have life—life in all its fullness. So even though this non-existent connection left a hole in my story, I believe God had a plan and purpose for my life. And although I didn't fully understand it then, that hole would eventually be filled by forming strong bonds and cultivating genuine connections that would position me to prosper.

Then, even if your beginnings were modest, your final days will be full of prosperity.

—Job 8:7 CSB

The dictionary defines *prosper* as being successful or fortunate; to flourish; to thrive. In my mind, it's impossible to define the word *prosper* without talking about relationships. There is scientific proof that we are not here to live this life alone. We are wired for connection. For me, defining prosper means taking any dictionary definition and adding the words *in relationships* to the end. Prospering is about being successful or fortunate in relationships. It is about growing strong and healthy, finding fulfillment, thriving, and flourishing...in relationships.

As I write this chapter, I am reminded of the divine revelation represented in its title: "I Woke Up Like This." It isn't just about the physical act of rising from a night's sleep each morning. This chapter is an exploration of a series of awakenings. An ever-evolving journey from the day I entered this world, to some of the impactful relationships that formed a buffer around me and guided me through life to the profound, yet gradual realization of my purpose. I am reminded of countless moments where the simple act of being in community with others was transformational—for me and those around me.

During my next awakening—I call it my re-awakening—I woke up to the realization that when I flourish, I help others flourish. I was an intern at a local middle school completing my fieldwork to earn my master's degree. It was the beginning of the fall semester, and I was slated to graduate in December. I'd heard that one of the school counselors was retiring soon. I spoke to the counseling director, who by now I considered a mentor. She helped me muster up the courage to schedule a meeting with the principal to see if I could get an interview. I sat down in the principal's office, and I can remember her chewing a piece of chocolate and breathing audibly through her nose. She smiled at me and kindly said, "No, baby, you won't have your license in time. I can't hire you." I could feel the heat in my face as I shrunk inside. How did I think I was about to get the hookup?

I Woke Up Like This

December came, and I graduated. In February, I got wind of another school counselor position opening at a middle school on the same side of town. I applied, got the interview, and they offered me the job. Yes! I'd landed my first big-girl job. I could cruise through the next few months with confidence knowing that come August, I'd have a full-time job with benefits! I stayed at the school for five years. Supporting my three-hundred-plus students for all three of their middle school years, I was able to nurture our relationships. I learned *all* their names. I learned to be fully present and listen to their hearts. By being fully engaged, I earned their trust and gained a better understanding of their trials and tribulations and their hopes and dreams. I became their bridge builder, confidence igniter, and mindset motivator. I was on fire! That hole was getting smaller and smaller. I was flourishing, and so were they.

"Deep listening is the kind of listening that can help relieve the suffering of another person. You listen with only one purpose: to help him or her to empty their heart."

— Thich Nhat Hanh

One of my sixth graders worked hard to find her place and identity in the new middle school with students converging from six different elementary schools. She was in my office a lot! I'm not sure what happened, but one day, she ran out of the building into the field behind the school. The counseling director went out, the administrator went out, they even sent the school resource officer out, and this child would not budge. Finally, they called me. I went out to the line where the field met the concrete. I can't remember the whole conversation, but I told her there were snakes in that field. and there was no way I was coming out there. If she wanted to talk to me, she needed to follow me to my office—now! She stood there for a while. I turned around and never looked back. A few minutes later, she

57

entered the building and came to my office, leaving a trail of mud from the field. The more we talked, the more she opened up.

That day, I listened as she poured out her heart. I wanted her to feel seen, heard, and understood. She became one of my frequent flyers, and together we conquered middle school. Now she is a grown woman. Not only are we still connected, but she also attended my wedding, has babysat my children, gone on vacation with us, and now I get to call her Soror as she is a member of my sorority. At any gathering, you can find us telling stories of the impact we had on each other during her middle school years. These bonds were formed with many of my students in that cohort. I immersed myself in their culture. I did all the things to ensure that, although I was their elder, I was authentic, relatable, trustworthy, and accepting of the person they were versus the person they sometimes had to pretend to be.

"I've learned that people will forget what you said, people will forget what you did, but people will never forget how you made them feel."

— Maya Angelou

By my second year, the staff shifted, and I found myself a part of the best counseling team. You know when a whole department eats lunch together every day, we must actually like each other. There were five of us, and all our birthdays were in March or April. The Rolfe Crew, as we still call ourselves, became my circle of support. Even though I was the youngest and least experienced, they made me feel like a giant in the field. They mentored me, listened to me, and guided me with total acceptance. But they also gave me the autonomy to be creative and develop my own programs.

And when I finally found Mr. Right, they supported me during his deployment, helped plan my wedding, and moved me into our new home. Those were the best years of my adult career. They provided unconditional support, pouring into me as I poured into my students.

So, when I was five years in, the school counseling director position was about to open as my boss was set to retire. She poured into me all those years, intentionally preparing me for her position. I was a fav among teachers and staff, so we thought this would be easy. I interviewed, knocked it out of the park, and a few days later found out they gave the job to someone else. I'm not going to tell you how that story ended. But I will tell you that another director position was open at a nontraditional school nearby, and it had my name on it.

One day I received a call from Central Office. The person on the phone asked, "Are you going to apply for the position at the nontraditional school?"

In my slight rage, I replied, "No. You know I was supposed to get that job." After some back-and-forth and her convincing me how great I would be for that position, I decided to apply, interviewed, and got the job.

Within my first year, my principal left, and I found out that the principal from the middle school who wouldn't hire me back in grad school would be the interim principal. One day I was in her office and decided to ask, "Do you remember me? I asked for a position at your school, and you wouldn't give me the job. Do you know I ended up at Rolfe?"

Her reply was one I will never forget. She said, "Yes. How do you think you got that job?"

I'm getting chills right now as I do every time I tell this story.

That day, I woke up to the realization that we all need to be connected to people who are flourishing and will help you flourish, who will mention your name in rooms you don't yet have access to.

The idea of flourishing based on material assets, money, education, and status has never really been my thing. But flourishing through relationships allowed me to prosper from the inside out, and all those other things were by-products of those relationships. Every encounter, every conversation, every shared moment played a crucial role in shaping the woman I was becoming.

My husband was in the military, and after six years of being at the same duty station, he received his orders. In 2011, we moved from Virginia to Davenport, Iowa. It wasn't hard to adjust as we both belong to Greek letter organizations, which means there is nowhere we can go and be a stranger. On our second day in town, we bumped into a sorority sister while out having lunch. She offered to take me to the next chapter meeting and get my husband connected to his fraternity brothers. Just like that, we were connected! Those bonds would make our three-year stay one to remember.

After several months of getting acclimated, my husband suggested that I join him in being a mentor with Big Brothers Big Sisters of the Mississippi Valley. I'd been a Big Sister back in Virginia, so I was familiar with the process. Our babies were both under three years old, and I was struggling a bit with the whole stay-at-home-mom thing. This was not my MO! I was trying to find purpose in my new life, so I said yes. I remember the first time I met my Little Sister. She was thirteen or fourteen at the time—cute brown-skinned girl with a birthmark on her face. She looked like she had a lot on her mind, but she smiled, we talked, and made plans to get together.

For the next two years, our bond was strengthened. We had consistent outings. I would take her to enriching events and expose her to leadership opportunities. We had a blast. I always knew there was a lot going on at home, and I hoped in some way our relationship would be a safe space where she could be her authentic self and realize that becoming her best self was possible.

I Woke Up Like This

Recently, I was scrolling through Facebook, and I saw a post that said, "I miss my family and friends!" It was my little sister from Iowa.

I commented, "Hey Girl Hey...Sending Love (with a heart emoji)."

Her response, "I miss you the most."

This led to a few exciting DMs and an exchange of new numbers. I called her on a Sunday evening. For an hour, we reminisced about our Big Sister, Little Sister time together. She recalled moments I'd totally forgotten about. She said she was glad to have this opportunity to give me my flowers. She proceeded to tell me that I had no idea how much our time meant to her, and that her childhood was a struggle. She looked forward to our outings. Every time we got together was a time away from the chaos, and it helped her make it through some tough times. I had to share with her, too, how I grew so much through our relationship and that it meant so much to me to be a safe space for her. I woke up to the fact that I needed to be the connection that I needed.

I was on 95 South heading home and decided to finish a podcast that I started earlier on the way to work. Within the first ten minutes, I heard a voice coming from my car speakers, clearly say, "Someone's breakthrough is waiting on you!" I think I had crochet braids at the time, but I can say these words literally blew my hair back! I looked in my rearview mirror and in the passenger seat. God, is that you? Clearly, he was on the road with me that day. In my talks with God, I always asked Him to send me signs that I couldn't miss. I'd been through these enough times to know when a sign was *the* sign. I was excited and nervous all at once. I wanted desperately to be in alignment with Him. This would be the start of what I called my re-reawakening where I'd find out how flourishing in connections would lead me to my purpose.

"History will judge us by the difference we make in the everyday lives of children."

— Nelson Mandela

The year the pandemic hit, my word for the year was *clarity*. It was almost the end of the year, and I still needed to hear from God as to what was next. This was also about this time when I received an invitation to join a virtual group coaching program. I accepted and somehow was blessed with two individual "sessions" with our coach. Each conversation was God-ordered moments with her that grew to be life changing. In those conversations, we processed my ideas, and it quickly became clear to me that I wanted to serve teens and young adults through life coaching.

I went on to earn my certification. Having no entrepreneurial experience, I found my circle of support—a business startup and networking space for black and brown women. I followed all the steps and did all the things, and in February 2021, Unbreakable Minds Coaching was born! My mission: to help young people change their mindset, so they meet the best version of themselves and live their best life with purpose on purpose.

The ink was barely dry on my certificate. I posted it on Facebook. I received lots of congrats and "Can you show me how you did that?" and one inquiry about my services. I remember the discovery call like it was yesterday.... I had all my documents. I wanted to sound qualified and be prepared to answer any question that came my way. None of that mattered. My relationship with this mom had been nurtured through a previous encounter. She knew that I had a solution to her problem—"My son and my daughter need you. Sign them up!" I had my first two clients! For three years, the daughter and I flourished together. She is still my client and mentee and a college student who continues to prosper.

My business began to take flight as community members, small business owners, and program providers were drawn to my mission. A whole new circle of support was forming around me. However, with the idea of success came new fears. Elevating as a solopreneur was scary and even lonely at times. I knew the why and the what, but the how felt risky. In all my awakenings, I had never been a risk taker. I always wanted to feel like I was in control, only entering new endeavors that felt safe.

This time, I woke up to letting fear be my guide and having faith to stand back and watch God work. In my re-reawakening, I came in alignment with His plan, and everything I was looking for found me. I was no longer a solopreneur. God was my CEO, and He blessed me to share this space with my husband, who was also led to coach young people. Our girls are watching as we build a legacy, guiding and nurturing young minds, pouring into them what has been poured into us.

I discovered that my power and purpose had been within me all along. I'd been looking for lights, camera, action, but the truth became clear: just show up and be me. Once I figured out that connecting was my superpower, my natural gifts emerged: to change the energy in a room, to calm people with my presence, and to help them remove blockers so they could see their power shine through. I provided safety, built bridges, and ignited confidence. This was the key to leading my clients to their breakthrough.

Perhaps, like me, you have a hole in your story and are still healing. Or you are a bonafide introvert and you're looking at this page sideways thinking, "peopling" ain't really my thing. No matter who you are, how old you are, or what you've been through, you can do this! You too can maximize your ability to prosper by intentionally focusing on the connections in your life. I often text my husband and our girls in the morning to say, "Make today count." I'm basically saying be intentional to see what you can glean from every conversation, every interaction, and every shared moment.

Here are eight tips you can implement to experience your own awakenings, leading you to a life of connection, purpose, and prosperity:

1. Reflect on your early life experiences. Become aware of what circumstances have shaped your mindset about the world and your place in it.
2. Wake up each day, not just physically, but also mentally and spiritually, intentionally looking for opportunities to connect, learn, and grow.
3. Embrace God's plan for you, understanding that whatever you need will find you.
4. Believe that you were born to prosper, and each stage of your life has prepared you for this moment in time.
5. Connect with people who are flourishing and can help you flourish. Seek out mentors and supporters who will mention your name in rooms you don't yet have access to.
6. Identify your tribe—people you feel safe to fail around, who have your back, believe in your vision, and will stand ten toes down for you, no matter what. This may or may not include family and that's okay!
7. Recognize the simplicity of your purpose—just show up as your authentic self.
8. Realize that when you flourish, you help others flourish. Notice how your growth positively impacts those around you.

Use these tips as a guide to help you navigate your own journey of self-discovery and growth. Embrace each awakening as a step toward fulfilling your purpose and prospering in life, career, and business.

I'll end with this: Relationships are the new currency. Just like capital gains, the connections we invest in compound over time, growing in value and enriching our lives. Every meaningful interaction pays dividends in the form of trust, support, and mutual growth. The equity we build in our relationships provides a foundation of strength and stability, enabling us to weather life's challenges. Bonds are the ties that bind us together, offering security and resilience.

As you navigate your journey, remember that flourishing through relationships is the ultimate investment. Nurture your connections with the same care and attention you would give to any valuable asset. By doing so, you'll find that the returns are immeasurable.

If you look for meaning in your relationships, your relationships will become more meaningful!

I hope getting a peek at my journey will inspire you. I woke up like this, and I'm believing the same for you too!

Meet the Author | Yolanda W. Hall, BS, MEd, CLC

Yolanda Hall is a dedicated professional hailing from Queens, New York, now residing in Chester, Virginia. A graduate of Virginia Commonwealth University, Yolanda has devoted more than twenty years to empowering and guiding young minds toward discovering their greatness. Her extensive experience spans roles such as school counselor, school counseling director, and prevention coordinator, which have seamlessly paved the way for her current endeavor as a certified mindset coach specializing in working with youth and families.

In 2021, Yolanda founded Unbreakable Minds Coaching with a mission to help teens and young adults change their mindset so they can meet the best version of themselves and live their best life with purpose on purpose. Her coaching services cater to individuals and groups aged fifteen to twenty-five, providing support not just to the youth but also to parents and professionals in youth-serving organizations, fostering nurturing relationships and safe spaces.

Known for her magnetic presence, Yolanda is celebrated for her ability to create a safe, calm, and inclusive atmosphere where individuals feel seen, heard, and understood. Her influential work extends into the community through initiatives like Teen Table Talks, The Queens Court (for high school girls), Mother Daughter Circle, Unbreakable Moms Night Out, and Parenting on Purpose Workshop Series.

Professionally, Yolanda serves as an environmental strategies coordinator, following a distinguished tenure as a prevention coordinator where she facilitated a NACo award-winning community-based program. Her prior experience includes fifteen years as a school counselor serving middle and high school students. This includes three years serving military-connected youth, where she established the Smith Ambassadors Program, identifying and training students with untapped potential to become school leaders and supportive guides for new students.

Yolanda, wanting to shine a light on equity, diversity, and inclusion, initiated the No Place for Hate program in her middle school, which earned the governor's recognition in 2017 and 2018. The third year, Yolanda helped infuse this program into all twelve middle schools in the district. Additionally, she was nominated by her school staff for the Christie Award, which recognizes a support services staff member who has been exemplary in their service to students and families.

Yolanda is an adverse childhood experiences (ACE) interface master trainer and is accredited to facilitate various trainings including Adult Mental Health First Aid, Activate Your Wellness, AFSP Talk Saves Lives, NAMI Ending the Silence, and One Circle Foundation programs. An active member of Delta Sigma Theta Sorority, Inc., she also fulfills roles as a youth and young adult counselor and marriage mentor at St. Paul's Baptist Church, and as a board member of the Live Red Foundation.

Outside her professional life, Yolanda cherishes her role as a wife and mother to two teenage daughters, enjoying family time, travel, and live performances. Through her work and personal endeavors, Yolanda Hall exemplifies a commitment to her community and a passion for making a lasting impact on the lives of others.

Learn more by visiting
https://linktr.ee/unbreakablemindscoaching.

The Rhythm Within
Wanda Washington

Empathy Understanding

In life, there exists a profound rhythm, a steady pulse that resonates deeply within each of us. "A strong, regular, repeated pattern of movement or sound." This rhythm, a testament to the presence of life, persists even now, echoing within my being. It's the familiar vibration of my daughter's heartbeat. A beautiful melody, that rises above mere biology. When I first held her, feeling each rhythmic beat against my palm, I was drawn into a profound connection, a connection that intertwined her journey with mine. Little did I realize that I was being transformed into a higher calling. Through her heartbeat, from her essence to my very fingertips, I crossed a path illuminated by divine purpose. Join me now as I extend an invitation to Anna's sanctuary, a place where the essence of love unfolds and flourishes, a haven where the pulse of life beats the strongest.

Resilience and Growth

On Friday, November 13, 1992, a date that continues to haunt me, I found myself rushed to the hospital, far too early into labor, eagerly awaiting the arrival of our precious baby girl.

As I arrived at the hospital and settled into a wheelchair, my doctor approached with a grave expression, looking at me with a stern gaze. "This baby is going to die," she declared, her words landing like a ton of bricks. Swiftly shifting into recovery mode, I pressed for a C-section.

"No, it would be bad for you," became her firm response.

Confusion swirled within me. What did she mean, no? I was at a loss, unsure how to challenge this decision.

Despite feeling every flutter and kick within me—unmistakable signs of life—I wrestled with disbelief and uncertainty. The doctor affirmed the strength of her heart and the consistency of her movements. She was alive. Holding on to that rhythmic assurance became my lifeline, a beacon of hope among the doctor's bleak prognosis. I resolved to match the resilience of her heartbeat, determined not to succumb to tears or emotional anguish.

Throughout my pregnancy, I believed that my baby experienced my emotions with equal intensity. If I cried, she would feel it, too, as if it were her own. She was preparing herself for the world beyond the womb, so I clung to that bond, steadfast in my determination to hold her in my arms, whole and healthy.

In those moments, I reflected on the dreams my husband, Tony, and I had made for our daughter. His desire to name her Toni. Envisioning a future where she would join a girls' basketball team dubbed "Tony the Tigers" coached by him and his brother Cory made me smile. We agreed to name her Antoinette Marie Washington. He could call her Toni his whole life. Yet, as her arrival drew near, my hope was met with heartbreak. Her tiny form, silent and still, shattered our dreams in an instant. As I peeled back the blanket, revealing her fully formed features, a striking resemblance to her father emerged—those thick eyebrows, the unmistakable "Washington family trait," and the contours of a beautifully structured face. But it was when I glimpsed those delicate, pretty, perfect little feet that the floodgates of emotion burst open within me.

A primal scream tore from the depths of my soul, echoing through the sterile halls of the hospital with a raw intensity that drew the attention of those nearby. It was a cry of anguish, of disbelief, a howl of grief that demanded to be heard. So loud was my outcry that a concerned lady from the third floor ventured down to offer her condolences, a gesture that underscored the magnitude of our loss.

During my turmoil, my father arrived bearing comfort in the form of greens, chicken, and cornbread from my grandmother, prepared by her loving hands. Despite the love and support surrounding me, I remained trapped in a numbness that defied expression. My mother stood by, offering silent solidarity, her hand a steady anchor amid the storm raging within me.

The first time the nurse approached me seeking a name, I quickly declined. At that moment, I was not ready to make a quick decision. I needed time, she'd just died, I needed a minute. Losing her was too painful to give her name Antoinette to the wall of death—a name that represented so much life ahead. I was in deep denial and not ready to face the reality of her passing. The next day, the nurse brought me a picture of her named Baby Girl Washington and gently expressed the hospital needed a name for the death certificate. Upon reflection, I began to recognize the truth in her words. The death certificate represents a way to honor her existence and the significance of her brief time with us—a gesture of love and respect for the precious life that had graced our world. And so, with a heavy heart but a newfound sense of purpose, I gifted her a new name, Anna Marie, a testament to the depth of our love and the legacy she left behind, and a new identity in heaven.

As everyone around me urged me to move on and resume my life as if nothing had happened, I couldn't help but feel a deep sense of resentment. Their well-meaning reassurances of "You can have another one" only highlighted their lack of understanding of the profound emptiness that now engulfed me. Her life wasn't something that could be replaced. It held immense meaning, and at that moment, I needed the space to honor her memory, to mourn all the moments we would never share. I withdrew into silence, enveloped by the heaviness of my own grief, desperately clinging to the memories of her brief presence in my life.

An Angel Appears

I returned to work a week later, my mind swirling with questions about why this tragedy had unfolded and why it had to happen on Friday the thirteenth of all days. The date haunted me, leaving me grasping for answers. As I sat alone in the lunchroom, lost in my thoughts, a stranger approached—a woman I had never seen before. She took a seat beside me and uttered words that would forever change my perspective: "Friday the thirteenth is a blessed day." With that enigmatic statement, she rose and departed, leaving me to ponder the significance of her words.

Her unexpected insight provided me with a new lens through which to view my circumstances. Suddenly, I began to experience a profound sense of peace so intense that it scared me. How could I find peace while in such pain? Yet, as I delved deeper into this newfound tranquility, I realized that from loss can emerge personal growth and resilience, the ability to endure and rebound from life's most challenging trials.

With a renewed determination to heal, I decided to uproot from Portland, Oregon, and relocate to Atlanta, Georgia. Little did I know I was merely fleeing from my pain, not confronting it. It would take another eleven years before I truly embarked on the journey of healing that awaited me.

Power of Vulnerability

On February 21, 2003, I found myself yearning for closure, a necessity for my healing journey. To confront the traumas of my past head-on, I turned to the simple act of writing. With pen in hand and paper before me, I poured out every emotion, every feeling, every reaction that had been buried deep within. As the ink flowed, what emerged was nothing short of a beautiful love story.

Contemplating what to call this unexpected narrative, the image of a dove gracefully fluttered into my mind. Doves, renowned symbols of peace, spirituality, hope, renewal, transformation, and love, seemed to encapsulate the essence of my experience perfectly. And so, "A Dove" it shall be. Dear Anna, your life story is called "Crystal Dove."

Wanda Washington

* * *

Crystal Dove

She reminds me of a crystal dove
when I see her, I see love
I thank the heavenly stars above
for this innocent, precious child of God
Her life was ever bittersweet
but Lord she had a strong heartbeat
The heart of life—a mother's strive
To bring forth a child—she fought a good fight
The strike of death—a sign of life
A lie—the Truth
God's by my side
Save my child—the mother cried
Heaven-bound God replied
Pretty perfect little feet
This child of God has a strong heartbeat
The best of her is the best of me
This child of God will always be
She reminds me of a crystal dove
When I see her, I see love
I thank the heavenly stars above
For this innocent precious child of God

In Loving Memory
Anna Marie Washington (Toni)
November 13, 1992

Reflections of Love

After writing such a beautiful love story, I started to reflect on the man who would become her father, wishing he was here to share this pivotal moment in time—the love of my life. Let's journey back in time and explore a crucial moment as we witness the blossoming of our love story.

Sometimes a woman's thoughts may silently echo, whispering, "Step to me, my valentine, for a black man's love is divine." Well, I encountered the real deal. It happened at a bustling business event, where amid the crowd, a tall, slender man caught my eye, a vision of charm with a camera in hand.

As he approached my booth, he started to take my picture. A playful energy ignited between us. I posed and twirled, and laughter filled the air. With confidence, he stepped forward, extending his business card and introducing himself as Tony Washington, advertising executive for *The Portland Observer* newspaper.

"May I have your number?" he asked. His sincerity shone through with a smile. I shared my digits.

That evening, Tony reached out, setting the stage for our first dinner date on the following day. But before heading to our meal, he proposed a detour, a stop at the newspaper office of the family business. There, I met his mother and was greeted with warmth and kindness that left a lasting impression.

A mere week later, Tony officially asked me to be his girlfriend, marking the beginning of our journey together. And just a year after that, he took things a step further, presenting me with a ring and asking for my hand in marriage. Our love story continued to unfold, and then the following year brought the joyful anticipation of Anna's arrival.

Anna is with God and has everlasting life. From her hand to our hearts, we're proud of you, Toni.

Life Lessons

Despite the love I shared with my husband, I found myself navigating life without him, a journey I hadn't anticipated embarking on. While there's a common adage suggesting that time heals. I've come to realize that healing is an ongoing process with no set timeline. It's important to acknowledge and embrace every emotion as it surfaces, allowing oneself the space and time to process them in their unique way. Each individual finds motivation and strength in different ways to navigate daily life. For me, it involved allowing myself to confront and express the emotions I was dealing with. With the myriad of experiences I've encountered, I don't possess a definitive roadmap to offer others. Everyone's journey through grief and healing is deeply personal and unique. I can only share my coping with loss, learning, and evolving through my grief while continuing to nurture my capacity for love. There are no absolute rights or wrongs in how one deals with loss and copes with life's challenges. Navigating through grief has taught me invaluable lessons about resilience and the complexities of human emotions. As I continue to navigate this journey of healing and growth, I've come to rely deeply on my support system.

Support System

My three-tier support system forms a triangle, anchoring my foundation with unwavering support. "Triangles are the strongest shape there is." They distribute weight evenly on all three sides, showcasing resilience and balance. At the base lies the center, representing equilibrium in life's journey. While the weight may shift, the foundation remains unbroken. Just as the tip of the triangle points toward the sky, symbolizing growth and aspiration, my rock comprises my best friend, mother, and father. They form the base of my support system, anchoring me through life's storms.

The value of a good friend cannot be overstated. Since the seventh grade, I've been fortunate to have a friend with whom I could share anything. Her unwavering presence during the loss of my child provided invaluable support along the way.

In terms of my family, my mother remains my guiding light, both then and now. Her humble and gentle nature offers an immeasurable wellspring of support. Meanwhile, my father's words and wisdom serve as a source of inspiration. He encouraged me to embrace life's beauty by taking alternate routes, stopping to appreciate nature's wonders—blooming flowers, oxygen-producing trees, and the innate love of animals. His ability to uplift others through the lens of nature. A true lover of the outdoors, my dad's meticulously groomed yard became a haven for every creature in the neighborhood—dogs, cats, birds, and more—drawn to its peaceful and safe atmosphere, much like the sanctuary he provided for me. His teachings fostered a profound awareness of the interconnections of all living things, each playing a vital role in God's grand design of flourishing in life, growth, and abundance.

My parents serve as the ultimate blueprint for flourishing in every aspect of life, be it personal, professional, or entrepreneurial. Despite humble beginnings on a farm, they exemplified hard work, dedication, and the importance of core values. While prosperity often conjures images of wealth, for them, it was about flourishing in life.

It's crucial to define what prosper means on a personal level and create a balance that aligns with our own values and priorities. Both my parents epitomized a strong work ethic. My mother, a remarkable example, raised eight children and then pursued her dream of becoming a teacher. It demanded focus, endurance, perseverance, and an unwavering belief in her abilities to earn a degree while raising a large family. Her career choice may not have been financially lucrative, but it brought her immense happiness and fulfillment.

Conversely, my father's brilliance lay in his hands and mind. He engaged in thought-provoking conversations that challenged perception and delved into life's complexities. From a young age, he displayed a serious yet curious nature, even trailing ants to uncover their journey. Skilled in craftsmanship, he possessed the remarkable ability to transform old, discarded items into refined treasures. For instance, he once bought a dilapidated shack and, through his craftsmanship, transformed it into a magnificent mansion. His knack for seeing value in the existing inspired me deeply.

In essence, my parents' journey embodies the essence of true prosperity, a blend of hard work, resilience, creativity, and an unwavering commitment to flourishing in every facet of life.

For anyone striving to navigate the journey of personal growth, especially in the wake of the profound grief of losing a child, authenticity is paramount. Grief, encompasses a spectrum of emotions that wave back and forth, like a tide at sea that flows over time. It's crucial to honor your feelings, values, and inner spirit without inhibition. When trauma knocks at your door, it's okay to allow yourself to feel and process those emotions without suppression.

Maintaining strong family bonds can serve as an anchor, grounding you amid life's storms. These are the pillars that supported me during my darkest days. However, I also urge seeking professional help from a therapist who can provide invaluable guidance and support through this challenging journey.

Positive Transformation

As I search deeper into the meaning of the word *prosper,* I've come to understand that it encompasses more than just material success. It's about "pushing forward, passing through, and getting on" with a sense of purpose and fulfillment. This spiritual perspective resonates deeply with me, especially as I reflect on my journey as a wife, mother, and business owner. However, thriving in all aspects of life requires more than just following the heart's desires. It involves striking a delicate balance between passion and practicality, all while upholding values of integrity and care. Drawing inspiration from biblical teachings, according to Proverbs 11:25, *"A generous person will prosper, whoever refreshes, will be refreshed."* I see the term *prosper* as intertwined with peace, happiness, and well-being, a concept that transcends mere financial gains. With this perspective in mind, I recognize the importance of establishing a solid business plan and implementing effective marketing strategies to ensure sustained success in both life and business endeavors.

A business plan serves as a comprehensive roadmap for your business, projecting its trajectory over the next three to five years and outlining the strategies necessary to generate revenue and foster growth. This document is indispensable for guiding decision-making, securing investments, and navigating potential challenges. A business plan is a written tool that provides a clear vision of the path your business intends to take, laying the groundwork for sustainable success.

Equally important is the role of marketing, which is centered on generating interest in your products or services. Through market analysis, research, and understanding the needs and preferences of your target audience, effective marketing endeavors to attract and engage potential customers. By creating compelling messaging that resonates with your ideal customer base, businesses can effectively communicate their value proposition and cultivate lasting relationships. Ultimately, the purpose of marketing is not just to drive sales, but to establish a meaningful connection with customers and foster brand loyalty.

To ensure optimal success, it's essential to seek expert assistance in both crafting a solid business plan and executing strategic marketing initiatives. While innovative ideas may serve as the initial spark, it's the meticulous planning, execution, and expert guidance that lay the foundation for sustained prosperity in the future.

Success isn't just reaching a goal; it's a journey filled with choices, accomplishments, and triumphs. For me, success meant embracing the arrival of my daughter, Anna, who brought inspiration, motivation, and a deep lesson in love. Through her, I found purpose and direction, learning to lead with my heart while also using my mind wisely. This twofold approach to life and business allows me to prosper, moving forward with strength and clarity.

Meet the Author | Wanda Washington

Wanda Washington, the director and chief executive officer of Natural Beauty Boutique is dedicated to caring for your natural hair. Located in the picturesque Northlake area of Tucker, Georgia, Wanda brings twenty-one years of experience as a Sisterlocks™ educator and certified consultant. Additionally, she holds the title of master cosmetologist in the State of Georgia.

Wanda's journey through corporate training, team management, and state training in the telecommunications industry has equipped her with a diverse skill set encompassing customer service, business acumen, legal analysis, and claim servicing. In these roles, she played a pivotal part in mentoring service representatives, guiding them in handling client requests, understanding business needs, and devising effective strategies.

Now, as a customer care coach, Wanda seamlessly integrates her extensive background into her current responsibilities. Drawing from her wealth of experience, she not only imparts technical knowledge to Sisterlocks™ consultants, but also underscores the significance of client care methodologies. Her dedication to delivering excellence is evident in every facet of her work, reflecting the culmination of her past experiences and present role as a trusted guide in Sisterlocks™ training, and customer care.

Contact Information:

Natural Beauty Boutique LLC

For The Care of Your Natural Hair

2176 Henderson Mill Rd Ne, Loft 27

Tucker, GA 30345

Website: www.naturalbeautyboutique.com

Facebook: Wanda L Washington

Instagram: https://www.instagram.com/wanda2403/

A Journey of Healing to Prosper in Life and Business

Tanya Russell

Navigating life as a single mother presents an array of challenges, each demanding resilience, tenacity, and an unwavering commitment to the well-being of a child. I had my first daughter at the age of eighteen while in my first semester of college. This changed the trajectory of the plans I had for my future. I can remember being so afraid and unsure of what would lie ahead for us. The father of my child was not present, and this rejection made it even harder to deal with. At the age of thirty-two, I got married, and my journey took an unforeseen turn. In two years, I was going through a tumultuous divorce only to find myself a single parent again to my second daughter.

The end of my marriage not only shattered my world but also thrust me into a web of emotions from which I could not seem to get untangled. The intense pain of rejection, the sting of betrayal, and a profound sense of loss were evident in my daily walk. The responsibilities of single parenthood weighed heavily, further complicating my struggle to find solid ground. This period of my life was characterized by a sense of just being stuck, as if trapped within the confines of my own hurt and disappointments. Yet, it was within this web of pain that I began to unearth strengths I never knew I had. I began to take control of my thoughts and feelings. My relationship with my Lord and Savior Jesus Christ kept me centered knowing that through Him, I could conquer these feelings I'd carried for so many years. I learned invaluable lessons about resilience, forgiveness, and the spirit of a mother's love. This journey has been pivotal in shaping me into the woman I am today—stronger, wiser, ever-evolving—and I love who I've become.

The past was beginning to take its rightful seat behind me, and I started to see more clearly. It was evident that I had to dig deep and put in the work to build my confidence and self-worth. It was in this moment of profound vulnerability that I turned to my faith in God and therapy. My faith in God is the foundation upon which I began to rebuild my spirit through His Word. In quiet times of prayer and reflection, I began to see glimmers of the woman I was called to be. God had a plan for my life, and I could no longer stay entangled in my web.

Therapy provided the tools I needed to navigate the waters of the emotional traumas I experienced. Therapy provided a safe harbor where I could unload the burdens of my heart without fear of judgment. The decision to put myself first and do the hard work on me helped infuse a new sense of self-worth and acceptance. I can remember one evening during a session, I shared with my therapist how I felt so inadequate at times. I have a love for style and fashion, so I took great strides to look good on the outside, but inside, my self-confidence was shot.

She stared at me for a moment then said, "Tanya, you are so much stronger than you think."

This stuck with me. As I continued to lean on my faith and engage in therapy, a transformation began to unfold. After many years of carrying the burden of rejection, hurt, anger, fear, and low self-esteem, I gave myself permission to finally be free. I no longer held my heart hostage but allowed the breath of healing to take place and be reshaped into something new. I discovered a wellspring of confidence within me, a belief in my own resilience and in my capacity to begin anew. This confidence was not born out of a lack of wisdom but of a deep-seated knowledge that regardless of the trials I faced, I possessed the inner strength to overcome them. I learned to trust in the process, to embrace the knowledge that I am more than a conquer through Christ, and to view each day, not as a reminder of what was lost, but as an opportunity for growth and renewal.

Forgiveness. I learned forgiveness was not a concession to those who had wronged me, but a gift to myself. I likened it to a key that unlocked the chains of bitterness and pain that had ensnared my heart. Whatever you do, *do not* stay *stuck*.

In your journey to prosper in life, remember self-reflection and healing help to:

- acknowledge past rejections and hurts.
- understand their impact on your life and how to overcome them.
- determine whether to seek therapy or counseling if needed to heal emotional wounds. It's really okay.
- embrace forgiveness, both for yourself and others involved.

Embracing personal growth and healing became my new focus. I immersed myself in activities that nourished my soul and sparked joy within me. I sought out the company of those who uplifted and supported me, forging connections that were rooted in mutual respect and understanding. I learned to honor my needs and to set boundaries that protect my peace. I was slowly piecing myself back together, not as I once was, but working toward a better version of myself.

Healing, I realized, is not a destination but a daily journey of letting go of the baggage that keeps you weighed down. There are days when I feel as though I have regressed when the pain and doubt crept back in, threatening to undo all the progress I have made. Yet, it is in these moments that my faith in God and His Word reminds me, *"I can do all things through Christ who strengthens me"* (Philippians 4:13 NKJV).

Setbacks are simply a part of the healing process, lending opportunities to practice resilience and to deepen understanding of myself and strength. Learning to lean into this journey of growth and progress often brings tears to my eyes. I have come so far from that broken woman who thought she would never get to the other side. Being committed to God and my unwavering commitment to personal growth have been fruitful and rewarding. You can get to the other side too!

The dawning of my new beginning was taking place. In 2009, I relocated to North Carolina with my two daughters. This was an intentional move toward rebuilding my life. I wanted a fresh start. One such step was the decision to return to college. I promised my mother that I was going to finish college so she could see me graduate. This decision was not made lightly; it required a leap of faith, a belief in my ability to juggle the demands of parenthood, studies, and eventually, a new business venture. You see, I would be fifty years old at the time of graduation. College, for me, was not just about academic pursuit; it was a declaration of my commitment to myself, my children, and my professional development. I wanted them to see that no matter how old you are, it's never too late to pursue a dream. I was redefining my future and legacy.

I graduated from Shaw University with a bachelor of science degree in business administration with a concentration in management. It was always a dream of mine to become an entrepreneur and own my own business. While pursuing my degree, something unexpected happened: I met someone. One Saturday evening while relaxing at home, I received a text from a friend saying her husband's cousin saw a picture of me and inquired if I was single.

At this time in my life, I was not interested in pursuing a relationship with anyone, but after a background check through my friend and her husband, he sparked my interest, and numbers were exchanged. I lived in North Carolina, and he lived in Virginia, but despite the distance between us, work schedules, and my commitments at the time, we conversed daily over the phone. It became evident that we shared similar interests, goals, and most importantly, a love for God. After three months of talking over the phone and the anticipation of seeing each other in person, we had our first date and became inseparable.

An unexpected love blossomed—a new kind of love that grew quietly and steadily from a foundation of mutual respect, shared values and understanding of the scars we both carried. Our relationship has been a balm to my wounds of the past, offering not the illusion of perfection, but the promise of partnership of being seen and loved for who I truly am. God sent me his best, and we married in August 2018 and will be celebrating our sixth wedding anniversary this year. Together, we navigated the complexities of blending families and building a life that was not a continuation of what either of us had before but something entirely new.

My two daughters are adults now, and when I look at them, I feel so proud and blessed to be their mother. Their beauty, strength, and intelligence warms my heart. Our journey together has not been easy; the challenges we faced, and the scars of divorce left their mark. I can remember the nights I would cry silently in my room because I felt like I failed them and they deserved better. Watching them navigate the compass of their lives brings me much joy. They are both college graduates and are successfully charting their own paths, pursuing their passions and confidently building their futures.

I believe in order to prosper in my life and become an entrepreneur I had to begin from a place of healing and resilience to my personal hardships. Through my journey, I learned the importance of clarity—both in understanding my own values, my worth, and in envisioning the future I wished to create. This clarity of vision is indispensable in entrepreneurship. It guides decision-making, provides direction during times of uncertainty, and serves as a beacon for others who join you on your business journey. It's the foundation upon which a compelling brand story is built, one that will resonate with customers and distinguishes you in a crowded marketplace.

I believe my personal journey and my entrepreneurial journey go hand in hand. For me, building a business is not just about a vision or dream but a desire to create something meaningful to leave a mark on the world. What mark do you want to leave?

Bishop T.D. Jakes said, "If you can't figure out your purpose, figure out your passion," for your passion will lead you right into your purpose. My passion is to encourage, empower, and build confidence in women through style and fashion. Authenticity is key! No one can beat you being you. Authenticity in business is also about being true to your values, transparent in your operation and genuine in all transactions.

Today, I am the chief executive officer and owner of Styles By ChaVanni. We are a styling service and boutique that offers personal styling, personal shopping, closet refresh, and women's clothing. Our goal is to build confidence from the inside out through style and fashion. I believe gone are the days where we are dressed up on the outside but broken or full of turmoil on the inside. I know... I lived this before! My motto is "a well-dressed woman is one who is confidently dressed from the inside out."

Running a business can be overwhelming at times, but the key is to remain focused and stay on task.

A Journey of Healing to Prosper in Life and Business

Can I be transparent? I struggle in this area at times. The key, I discovered, is to prioritize tasks and the practice of self-care. Taking a step back to recharge is good to do. Also, staying focused means setting clear goals, breaking them down into manageable tasks, and celebrating each milestone, no matter how small. My journey, from personal adversity to entrepreneurial success is still being written, but it will be a story to the testament to the power of God, resilience, vision, empathy, discipline, authenticity, and innovation. Each of these qualities contribute to shaping an entrepreneurial mindset that is equipped to navigate the complexities of the business world. I am grateful for a loving husband, family, and my tribe who believe in me and support me. They are truly the sail that keeps me afloat.

As I reflect one last time on my own journey, I am reminded that the trials we endure are not merely obstacles to be overcome but are, in fact, the very experiences that prepare us for the challenges and opportunities we face in life and entrepreneurship. In sharing my story, I hope to inspire others to see their personal struggles not as detriments to their professional aspirations but as the very experiences that equip them to achieve greatness in their personal life and business. Prosper!

"You are not your history or your past. You are, however, what you choose to do with your present and future. The biggest breakthrough of your life will be when you realize that life truly happens from you and not to you."

— Dr. Cindy Trimm

Meet the Author | Tanya Russell

Tanya Russell, a native New Yorker, helps women professionals, entrepreneurs, and women in ministry to unlock and embrace their unique beauty and inspire confidence through their personal style. She believes the definition of a well-dressed woman is one who is confidently dressed from the inside and out.

Tanya attended the renowned Fashion Institute of Technology in New York City where she studied fashion buying and merchandising. She later went on to earn her bachelor of science in business administration: management from Shaw University. Today, while pursuing her entrepreneurial dream, she works in the corporate world of commercial banking. Tanya aspires to encourage, empower, and help women discover their own voice and purpose by sharing her life's journey. A young single mother at the age of eighteen, then going through a traumatic divorce, she was determined to turn her pain and disappointments into stepping stones to her purpose. Through her styling work, writing, and speaking, she has found her true calling.

In August 2022, Tanya became a first-time author of a book anthology entitled *Words of Wisdom for the Heart and Soul*. Tanya has also been featured in *Today's Purpose Woman Magazine*.

A Journey of Healing to Prosper in Life and Business

Tanya is a loving wife and mother of two amazing daughters and loves spending time with family and friends. She is the chief executive officer and founder of Styles By ChaVanni a women's styling service and boutique building confidence, one woman, one outfit at a time.

Ready to elevate your personal style? Connect with Tanya at thetanyadrussell.com.

Navigating Fear and Embracing Success

Prosper with a Corporate Mindset and Recognize Your Value

Sandy Weekes

I s fear preventing you from pursuing your dreams and goals? You're not alone. In today's fast- paced corporate world, overcoming fear and cultivating a corporate mindset are crucial for success. Join us as we explore the principles and practices that empower individuals to thrive in their careers, businesses, and lives by embracing collaboration, mentorship, and community.

Have you ever felt overwhelmed by fear, preventing you from pursuing your goals in business, life, or career? It's a common hurdle faced by many on a daily basis. Fear often holds people back from taking risks, pursuing their dreams, or achieving success in their careers. For women especially, focusing on our strengths and capabilities is essential for prospering in all aspects of life.

In today's dynamic and competitive corporate landscape, possessing the right mindset and recognizing one's value are crucial for personal and professional success. This chapter explores the principles and practices that enable individuals to thrive by cultivating a corporate mindset and understanding their intrinsic value while conquering fears in business, life, and career.

Understanding the Corporate Mindset

A corporate mindset encompasses attitudes, beliefs, and behaviors that align with the goals and values of the corporate world. It involves strategic decision-making, continuous learning, and prioritizing collaboration and teamwork.

Even as we achieve financial success and establish ourselves as business owners, the journey can still feel isolating. Regardless of our prosperity, there comes a point where we realize we can't surpass certain hurdles alone.

What I've come to understand is that successful entrepreneurs didn't achieve everything on their own. They recognize the power of collaboration in achieving prosperity. Success isn't about working alone but strategically partnering with others to achieve common goals.

I've learned that leveraging the expertise of others is essential for success in any business or career. Sharing the wealth in business, career, and life yields immense benefits. To prosper, we need to focus on key areas: support and community.

Support

We've all been there, thinking, *I can do this,* believing we can figure things out on our own. How many times have you uttered those words? How often have you found yourself spending hours searching for something online, convinced it's easier to do it yourself than to explain it to someone else? Over the years in business, I've learned that neglecting to invest in the right people has led me down a path of starting and stopping. It takes time, money, and energy to invest in the right person, in the right roles, and even in disrupting the team if they're not the right fit. Hiring the right person goes beyond just bringing in the support you need.

It's about allowing them a glimpse into your zone of genius, understanding how you operate, and assessing if they have your best interests at heart. If it's not the right fit, it leads to frustration, financial loss, and a lack of happiness and success. Every business owner desires to hire someone who can perform at their highest strengths and give their all. However, that's not always the case. The constant cycle of starting and stopping in business can be extremely frustrating.

I've learned that we have to be intentional with the hiring process. We need to know exactly what the responsibilities and tasks will be for the new hire. We should have standard operational policies in place, which would include the onboarding process, while we evaluate if this new hire is a good fit for what you need in your business right now. Hiring the right fits all at once can be overwhelming, so I suggest staging hiring. This gives us an opportunity to see what's missing now that we've hired three employees. It's essential to understand what is a good fit for our business. I've heard of clients who hired a virtual assistant, only to discover they were an excellent decluttering coach. They moved them into household chores, and the employee excelled in their genius.

Examine every area of your business, life, and career to see what you need right now. Who in your family can help you pick up additional tasks and household chores? What kind of support do you really need to ensure the business can function without you? If you have a nine-to-five job, who do you need to collaborate with in order for your projects to run smoothly? What are your career goals this month, and who can you rely on to help you achieve them? Maybe this isn't the time to hire six people, but one or two people might help you get the job done. Within the next quarter, focus and concentrate on your goals that you have to accomplish to be successful. In addition to hiring a person, invest in automation tools that will make your business life even simpler.

At this point in your business, you should know the tasks you will need to hire or outsource to an artificial intelligence, Fiverr, Upwork, or others. The goal is to prosper, and you need to determine what is needed to help you achieve your goals. There are many areas you have to evaluate to achieve your goals. You are in business to blaze new ground to achieve your prosperous goal. Start a conversation with other businesses about virtual assistants and staff members. See who they are using and who they would never use again. This is what I do—I don't reach out to family or friends. I ask business besties to share what they are hearing industry leaders chat about in the community. The good news is that you can start today without being a bother to others.

Building a solid support system is crucial for thriving in business, life, and career. Too often, we underestimate the power of having the right people by our side. Whether it's family members helping with household tasks or collaborating with colleagues at our nine-to-five job, the support we receive plays a vital role in our success journey.

By focusing on your immediate goals for the next quarter, you can streamline your hiring process and ensure that each addition to your team serves a specific purpose. Additionally, investing in automation tools can further simplify your business operations, freeing up your time to concentrate on strategic tasks.

Furthermore, networking with other businesses and industry leaders can provide valuable insights into the best practices for hiring and building a successful team. By tapping into the collective wisdom of your professional network, you can gain valuable recommendations and avoid potential pitfalls in the hiring process.

Remember, the goal is to prosper, and you have the power to shape your path to success. By taking a strategic approach to building your support network and leveraging the resources available to you, you can overcome obstacles and achieve your goals with confidence.

Community

Community plays a pivotal role in accessing prosperity and achieving success. At times, fear can manifest through judgment, distrust, and unworthiness, hindering our ability to connect with others. Personally, I underwent a transformative journey when a trusted friend took a different path, leaving me feeling isolated and distrustful. This experience compelled me to reassess my relationships and confront the fear that had crept into my life.

Through self-reflection and development, I identified the barriers holding me back and resolved to overcome them. Recognizing the significance of human interaction, I embraced the importance of community in today's fast-paced world.

Building a community isn't solely about promoting products; it's about fostering genuine collaborations and mutual prosperity. By delivering valuable content and facilitating meaningful interactions, we can create a supportive environment where members thrive in both their personal and professional endeavors.

Over time, I've learned that the quality of our community profoundly impacts our well-being. If dissatisfaction arises, it's essential to realign our focus and communicate openly with our members to ensure everyone is moving in the same direction.

Reflecting on past experiences, I've come to realize the power of authentic communication in fostering genuine connections. While automation may streamline processes, genuine human interaction remains invaluable in building strong communities and nurturing lasting relationships.

As we strive to prosper, let us remember the importance of community and the role it plays in our journey to success. By prioritizing meaningful connections and supporting one another, we can create a thriving community where everyone has the opportunity to flourish. Community serves as a cornerstone in achieving prosperity, enabling individuals to thrive in both personal and professional spheres, yet fear often obstructs our ability to connect authentically, breeding judgment and distrust.

My journey into the realm of community building was catalyzed by a pivotal moment when a trusted friend diverged from my path, leaving me grappling with feelings of isolation and apprehension. This experience compelled me to confront my fears head-on, reassessing the relationships and environments that surrounded me.

Through introspection and growth, I began unraveling the barriers that hindered my progress, recognizing the intrinsic value of human interaction in fostering a sense of belonging and support.

Building a community transcends mere transactional exchanges; it requires nurturing genuine collaborations and fostering an environment where mutual prosperity thrives. By delivering value and facilitating meaningful engagements, we pave the way for collective growth and fulfillment.

Over time, I've come to appreciate the profound impact of community on individual well-being. If discontentment arises, it's imperative to realign our focus and engage in open dialogue with community members to ensure alignment of goals and values.

Reflecting on past experiences, I've realized the irreplaceable nature of authentic communication in cultivating meaningful connections. While automation can streamline processes, genuine human interaction remains essential in fostering a sense of belonging and solidarity.

As we embark on the journey to prosperity, let us embrace the transformative power of community. By prioritizing authentic connections and fostering an environment of mutual support, we lay the foundation for collective success and fulfillment.

Navigating Fear and Embracing Success

Embarking on my entrepreneurial journey, I made a pivotal decision to enlist the guidance of a mentor. Recognizing the significance of learning from those who have traversed similar paths, I sought accountability and support to navigate the complexities of business, career, and life.

While I possessed the capability to chart my course independently, I embraced the wisdom of the buddy system, understanding its role in fostering safety and growth. Paired with someone with a few years of experience, I gleaned invaluable insights, avoiding pitfalls, and maximizing progress along the way.

Reflecting on my transition from the east coast to the west coast, I vividly recall the guidance of a seasoned librarian who illuminated the nuances of navigating library jurisdictions. This mentorship not only ensured my safety but also facilitated the achievement of organizational goals, fostering a thriving community within the library system.

Conversations with friends often prompt reflection on my steadfast commitment to investing in mentorship. While some question the need to seek guidance beyond books, I attest to the transformative power of accountability and community in propelling me toward success. Throughout my career, employers have championed my growth by facilitating access to top-tier mentorship and training. This investment in personal and professional development has equipped me with the mindset and skills necessary to foster meaningful connections and drive impactful change.

This chapter explored the principles essential for success in business, career, and life. Fear often acts as a barrier to achieving goals, but overcoming it and adopting a corporate mindset are crucial. Through collaboration, mentorship, and community, individuals can thrive and prosper in various aspects of their lives.

A corporate mindset encompasses attitudes, beliefs, and behaviors that align with the goals and values of the corporate world. It involves strategic decision-making, continuous learning, and prioritizing collaboration and teamwork.

Building a solid support system is crucial for thriving in business, life, and career. From family members helping with household tasks to collaborating with colleagues, the support we receive plays a vital role in our success journey.

Embarking on an entrepreneurial journey often requires guidance from mentors. Recognizing the significance of learning from those who have traversed similar paths, seeking accountability and support is key to navigating the complexities of business, career, and life.

Community serves as a cornerstone in achieving prosperity, enabling individuals to thrive in both personal and professional spheres. By prioritizing meaningful connections and supporting one another, a thriving community fosters an environment where everyone has the opportunity to flourish.

Prosper underscores the transformative power of overcoming fear and embracing a corporate mindset. Insights into collaboration, mentorship, and community highlight how individuals can overcome obstacles and achieve their goals with confidence.

By leveraging these principles and practices, readers are empowered to navigate the complexities of the modern corporate landscape. With a solid foundation in place, they can pave the way for a fulfilling and prosperous future. Success is not just about individual achievement but also about lifting others up and creating a supportive environment where everyone can prosper.

The Prosper Framework

In today's fast-paced and competitive world, achieving success in business, life, or career requires more than just talent and hard work. It demands a strategic approach, a resilient mindset, and a supportive network of allies. To guide individuals on their journey to prosper, I've created my Prosper Framework—a comprehensive blueprint designed to help individuals overcome obstacles, leverage opportunities, and unlock their full potential.

Understanding the Framework

At the heart of the Prosper Framework lies the recognition that true success is multifaceted, encompassing not only financial achievements but also personal fulfillment and holistic well-being. The framework consists of ten key elements, each addressing essential aspects of personal and professional growth:

Identify Your Fears: Fear is a common barrier that holds many individuals back from pursuing their goals and dreams. By identifying and acknowledging their fears, individuals can begin to confront and overcome them, paving the way for progress and success.

Cultivate a Corporate Mindset: Success in today's corporate world requires more than just technical skills—it demands a mindset characterized by strategic thinking, adaptability, and a commitment to continuous learning and improvement.

Recognize Your Intrinsic Value: Self-worth and self-belief are fundamental to success. Recognizing and embracing their inherent value, individuals can cultivate confidence, resilience, and a sense of purpose that propels them forward.

Build a Support System: No one achieves success alone. Building a strong support system of mentors, colleagues, and allies is crucial for overcoming challenges, navigating obstacles, and capitalizing on opportunities.

Nurture Authentic Connections: Authentic relationships built on trust, respect, and mutual support are essential for personal and professional growth. By fostering genuine connections within their communities, individuals can access valuable resources, insights, and opportunities.

Seek Mentorship and Guidance: Learning from the experiences and wisdom of others can accelerate personal and professional growth. Seeking out mentors and guidance allows individuals to benefit from the lessons learned by those who have traveled similar paths before them.

Embrace Change and Adaptability: In today's rapidly changing world, the ability to adapt and thrive in the face of uncertainty is essential. Embracing change, remaining flexible, and adopting a growth mindset are critical for navigating challenges and seizing new opportunities.

Take Action and Persist: Success requires more than just good intentions—it demands

action and perseverance. Setting clear goals, developing actionable plans, and maintaining a steadfast commitment to progress are key ingredients for achieving desired outcomes.

Give Back and Pay It Forward: True prosperity is not just about personal gain—it's also about making a positive impact on others and contributing to the greater good. By giving back to their communities and supporting others on their journeys, individuals can create a ripple effect of positive change.

Reflect, Refine, and Renew: Continuous reflection and self-assessment are essential for growth and improvement. By regularly evaluating their progress, refining their strategies, and renewing their commitment to excellence, individuals can ensure they stay on course toward their goals.

Implementing the Framework

Implementing the Prosper Framework requires a combination of self-awareness, strategic planning, and intentional action. Individuals can begin by reflecting on their current circumstances, identifying areas for growth and improvement, and setting clear goals for themselves.

From there, they can leverage the framework's ten key elements to develop personalized strategies and action plans tailored to their unique aspirations and challenges. Whether it's overcoming fears, building a support system, or cultivating a growth mindset, each element offers valuable insights and practical tools for success.

Throughout their journey, individuals should remain open to feedback, embrace opportunities for learning and development, and celebrate their progress and achievements along the way. By staying focused, resilient, and committed to their goals, they can navigate the Prosper Framework with confidence and clarity, ultimately realizing their full potential and achieving lasting success in business and life.

Meet the Author | Sandy Weekes

Sandy Weekes, co-author of *Prosper: A Guide to Flourish in Life, Business, and Career,* is a seasoned entrepreneur and mentor with expertise in research and development, project management planning. Passionate about empowering others, Sandy shares practical strategies for navigating life's challenges and achieving success. Through her collaborative approach, Sandy inspires individuals to conquer fears, build supportive communities, and pursue their goals with confidence. With her guidance, readers are encouraged to embrace their potential, pursue their dreams, and create lives filled with purpose and abundance.

Visit sandraweekes.com to learn more.

A Journey of Resilience and Triumph

Sonya Chiles

Life is a journey filled with unexpected twists and turns. For some, the road is particularly rocky, marked by trauma, heartbreak, and adversity. Yet, despite the barriers that may come our way, it is possible not only to survive but to thrive. This is the story of a curse breaker—a woman who is healing from the trauma of her past. A woman who has navigated through the darkest of times and emerged stronger, wiser, and more resilient than ever before.

My journey began as a spoiled grandchild, living a life only some would imagine. I was raised in an upper-middle-class neighborhood with quiet streets and beautiful homes. My grandparents raised me due to the shortcomings of my parents. My father was in and out of prison with a drug habit in tow. My mom was a young woman trying to figure it out who also experimented with drugs.

My grandmother was blessed with the opportunity to get it right one more time. She got the opportunity to raise me. She raised me with all the love and rearing she wanted to give to her children. She was a young mom with very little family, so raising her children was a "learn as you go "process.

And as for my grandad, they broke the mold when it came to that man, who married my grandmother with all seven of her kids and raised me. My grandmother didn't have to work or pay a bill. I never heard him raise his voice or tell any of us no. He was the epitome of love in my eyes, and I know I was the same in his.

Grandma always highlighted the good in people and never turned down anyone who needed help. If you needed a place to stay, you had it! If you needed to eat, you got it. She made you work for it now, but the reward outweighed the labor. My grandparents were truly a special pair. This was my foundation. This was where I learned to love unconditionally. But my understanding of what comes with unconditional love fell behind. My grandparents never explained to me the pain that came along with making others happy. They did what they thought was right. They truly loved.

As I grew, life started to happen, and things began to change fast. My grandparents felt the need to pass the parenting torch when I was twelve. This is when I moved in permanently with my parents, and boy, did things get dark. My teenage years were spent trying to figure out *why me?* Thoughts stirred through my head about the reasons why decisions were being made without my consideration. I was always taught to be seen and not heard, so what happened? The trauma was silenced, and the internal war began. I rebelled. I was defiant. I was suicidal. I was in pain. I wanted out. I navigated those years the best I could—navigated straight to a relationship with a gangster, a pregnancy at nineteen, and a prison wife at twenty.

Weed and alcohol took me through years of my pain. I was on my own with three children and refused to go back home for anything. I sold drugs and worked two jobs to provide for my kids, determined to provide a better life to them than my parents had for me. The wiser me understands that I was being more and more like my parents every day. In my fog, things were going well. In reality, I was on my way to possible jail time and losing my children. I was also in a prison relationship that caused a lot of stress and pain. I was swimming in misery. I became a hardened and careless shell of a being.

My face never showed my pain. Despite being a complete mess inside, I still mustered the strength to pour into others. When I did choose to share, people would respond with shock and little support.

"What do you mean you are sad?"

"Oh my God! But you look so happy!"

I knew people meant well, but those comments cut like a knife. I wanted and needed help, but I was afraid to ask for it. Mental illness was heavily stigmatized in the family, so there was no talking about it. You just simply let things simmer and forgive. This didn't sit too well with me. How can I forgive those who say they love me and hurt me? And I don't want anything to simmer but my food.

I started my interpretation of therapy with journaling. I began to write the things I wanted to say to others in my journal. Some of the entries were very dark, but I gave myself permission to be there. I reflected on the entries and how I felt during the process. It really helped me unpack my feelings without interruption or judgment. I felt I finally had something to trust.

Time passed on, and my grandfather took ill. This took the family by complete surprise. He had just retired and was diagnosed with pancreatic cancer. He hid it until he couldn't anymore. I watched one of the strongest men I knew wither away into nothing. I was so numb to what was going on, and it set me back mentally. I expected the family to be more than they were. I expected the same love he showed us to be given to him. It didn't happen like that. Grandpa passed leaving Grandma in a great financial position yet heartbroken. Four years later, she passed away.

When my grandparents passed, the family split, and suddenly I felt alone. I began to see family members and friends for who they really were. I started to seek help the best way I knew and felt hurt each time. Opening up to others is hard when you have hidden so many feelings and emotions for so long. I felt betrayed by those who I was raised to love and hold high regard. I began consuming myself more with my children and their activities. I stopped smoking weed and started to put the work in for my healing process. Despite the odds stacked against me, I was determined to create a better life for myself and those I loved.

Over time, I rekindled my relationship with my husband. We went seven years without speaking or seeing each other. The stress of the relationship was weighing heavily on my mental and physical health. This time, his maturity led me to feel like I could love and trust again. He had become my emotional support. He was everything I needed at the time. Our growing love inspired me to expand my love by helping other inmates and families of inmates as well. I founded a nonprofit organization to provide support to people like me, a prison wife. Through the journey, I met a lot of people and learned a lot of things. I could almost see my way out of the darkness.

The children were almost adults, and my life was beginning to change drastically for the better. I felt on top of the world being able to help those who have walked my path. The satisfaction of my service had covered the abandonment of the things I lost. I gained strength fighting for those who couldn't fight for themselves.

Time was approaching for my husband to finally come home, and the excitement was overwhelming. However, ten months after he came home, life threw me another curveball: a public marriage that ended in divorce. No matter how strong I pretended to be, I was left to navigate the complexities of the emotional fallout of a broken relationship.

The anger I had for what my ex-husband had done blocked my healing. The devil consumed my thoughts. I truly wanted revenge. I wanted to hurt him just as much as I was hurting, and to me, that meant he had to die. I felt this with every inch of my soul, but I couldn't move. God would not let me react in connection with my thoughts. It was a real-live battle going on between the devil and the God in me. And unfortunately, the devil was winning.

I had a moment of breakdown where God stripped my soul. I was hurt. I was angry. I laid in bed for as long as I could one day. Tears began to roll uncontrollably. Everything around me was dark in a room filled with sunlight. I struggled to make it into the bathroom, eyes filled with tears and heart racing. I turned on the shower and went in. I felt the power of my ancestors gathering and covering me. I felt God's presence and heard His voice speak to me. I fell into prayer. The water began to feel like bricks were falling on my back. I emerged from that shower feeling like I was a new person. I refused to be defined by my circumstances. Instead, I chose to listen to God and channel my pain into fuel for personal growth, finding solace in the power of self-reflection, forgiveness, and resilience.

With each setback I faced, I emerged stronger, more resilient, and more determined than ever before. Through the process of healing and self-discovery, I learned to embrace my past, recognizing that it was not a reflection of my worth or potential. I chose to focus on the present moment, seizing every opportunity for growth, connection, and joy. The most valuable lesson that I learned on my journey to prosperity was the importance of self-love.

I refused to buy into the narrative of self-doubt and insecurity. Instead, I made a conscious decision to prioritize my own well-being, cultivating a deep sense of self-compassion, acceptance, and gratitude. Through acts of self-care, mindfulness, and authenticity, I discovered that true happiness comes from within and that by loving myself fully, I was able to create a life of abundance and fulfillment.

Today, I stand with my head held high. I pride myself in raising my children, helping them graduate from school and being able to provide the emotional support they need to get through life. Self-awareness has taught me how to be true to who I am and not apologize for it. I can now look at myself in the mirror and say, "I'm proud of you, and I love you" without struggling and ending up in a ball of tears. I understand that life is a lesson, and the healing process never ends. The best thing is... I have understanding and that this is all I need to understand.

Today, I use my story as a powerful reminder that there is indeed life after trauma and that no matter what challenges we may face, we have the power to overcome them. Through resilience, courage, and unwavering determination, I have not only survived but thrived, proving that the human spirit is capable of incredible strength and resilience. My journey serves as a beacon of hope for all those who may be struggling, reminding us that no matter how dark the night may seem, dawn always brings the promise of a new day. It can be easy to lose sight of our own strength and resilience. It is in our darkest moments that our light shines brightest. By embracing our challenges, learning from our setbacks, and cultivating a deep sense of self-love and compassion, we have the power to not only survive but thrive.

Meet the Author | Sonya Chiles

Sonya Chiles is a beacon of resilience and empowerment, dedicated to guiding others through life's challenges with grace and tenacity. With years of experience as a motivational life coach, author, and entrepreneur, Sonya has cultivated a profound understanding of the human spirit and the power of transformation.

Sonya was born and raised in Richmond, Virginia. Her journey is a testament to the indomitable strength of the human spirit. She navigated the complexities of life, from the hardships of being a prison wife to the heartbreak of divorce, emerging stronger and more determined than ever.

Driven by her unwavering commitment to helping others, Sonya founded a nonprofit organization dedicated to supporting returning citizens from prison and their families. Through her nonprofit, she provides essential resources, guidance, and a beacon of hope to those navigating the challenging journey of reintegration into society.

As an author, Sonya's words resonate deeply with readers, offering solace, inspiration, and practical wisdom for navigating life's trials. Her books serve as guiding lights, illuminating the path to personal growth, resilience, and self-love.

With a heart full of compassion and a spirit that knows no bounds, Sonya continues to uplift and empower individuals from all walks of life. Her message is clear: No matter the obstacles, there is always hope, and within every individual lies the power to overcome and thrive.

In every word she speaks and every action she takes, Sonya Chiles embodies the essence of empowerment, resilience, and unwavering hope. Her life's work is a testament to the transformative power of belief in oneself and the limitless potential within us all.

To learn more about Sonya and everything she does, visit her website at www.sonyathesheeo.com.

Forty Acres and a Mule
Sharvette Mitchell

Can I be transparent with you? This chapter almost did not happen. The words of this chapter almost did not get written. Why? Because I stared at a blank screen with no inspiration or direction to go. For a short time, I second guessed whether I had enough to write. Specifically, could I really talk about the topic of prospering, advancing, flourishing, and prosperity? *Maybe I will just write the introduction of the book,* I thought.

Keep in mind, I am the visionary author, and I selected the book title! At the time of this book publication, I am in my seventh year of full-time entrepreneurship. This is my seventh book collaboration and anthology that I have spearheaded and led. I have hosted seven conference/summits and produced more than 745 podcasts/talk radio shows. And yet, I struggled with writing this chapter...

That's the funny thing about impostor syndrome. It's that sneaky feeling of doubting your own achievements, almost like you're playing a part in a play where you're the last to know you're the star. You might look around and think everyone else belongs, but somehow, you just got lucky or managed to fool everyone into believing you're better than you really are. Now, you might wonder, *Sharvette, you experienced this?*

Yes, and it turns out that anyone can be caught in this trap of self-doubt—from your seasoned professionals to high achievers who sometimes forget to internalize their successes.

I remember thinking about impostor syndrome while watching the documentary called, *I Am Bolt,* which is about Usain Bolt, a retired (2017) Jamaican sprinter widely considered to be the greatest of all time. At the moment this book goes to print, he remains the world record holder in the 100 meters, 200 meters, and 4×100 meters relay. Usain is an eight-time Olympic gold medalist and an eleven-time world champion.

With all of those accomplishments and gold medals hanging around his neck, he said he still questioned his ability before *every* race. He still wondered if he was fast, even with documented records that had not been broken... So, if you ever feel like an impostor, remember, you're not alone, and yes, you deserve your successes, you have credibility, and your voice is worthy of being heard.

FYI: That previous sentence was for me and not just for you. Just talking to myself.

I should mention that my other pause with this chapter was around which direction I would write. All of my six prior book collaborations —*PROPEL, POUR, PURSUE, PEARLS, Prepare for PURPOSE, and Positioned to PIVOT*—have been written with business advice or corporate strategies. I started to go in that same direction, but I could not. I could not talk about this topic of *"prosper"* without talking about faith and God. I just could not do it. Everything I have is because of God, and everywhere I am going will be because of God.

So, if you are looking for my normal professional development strategies and business vibes, they are still here but laced and intertwined with more personal stories and a dash of faith. I strongly believe that every business owner operates with some level of faith. You may not call yourself "faith-based," or you may not subscribe to a certain religion or faith, but if you wake up every day believing that your products will continue to sell and people will continue buying your services, that, my friend, is faith.

Let's first chat about what it means to be prosperous. It's not just the numbers in your bank account or the revenue hitting your business books (they absolutely matter). True prosperity is about flourishing in the corners of your life that matter to you.

1. In Life: Think about the moments that make you feel alive—the side-splitting laughs, the peace that comes with a deep breath, the small daily wins. That's where real prosperity lives. It's about the richness of your connections, the contentment in your heart, and the excitement that bubbles up when you think about the plans God has for your future and your loved ones.

2. In Business: Guess what? A prosperous business is a revenue-generating venture. It's also the smiles you create, the community you build, and the difference you make in customers' lives. It's the kind of success that echoes beyond your office walls, touching lives and lifting others up as it goes.

3. In Your Career: Climbing the career ladder, building your platform, or advancing your career to better raises and positions is always a good thing. Let's not forget prosperity is also found in the passion for your work, the respect you earn, and the knowledge you gather. It's in the meaningful impact you have and the life it allows you to build and create.

So here's the thing: Prosperity is deeply personal. It's not one-size-fits-all, and you can't measure it with a ruler. It's about setting goals that sing to your soul and taking the steps that resonate with who you are.

Because when you can look around and say, "This is my version of success," that's when you know you're prosperous. I challenge us all to embrace that full, rounded view of prosperity and make it our own, shall we?

I started thinking about where prosperity first started showing up in my life. What examples of prosperous mindsets were in my journey? I was drawn to think about my maternal great-grandmother Viola and my paternal grandmother Addie (we called her Granny).

Great-Grandmother Viola (Maternal)

My great-grandmother Viola worked at Georgia College in Milledgeville, Georgia. I am not sure what kind of job she had there, but it was during the 1940s. Great-grandmother Viola passed down two houses to her daughter, my maternal grandmother Mamie. My mother, Bettye, and her siblings lived in one of the houses. My mother lived there from nine years old until she went off to college.

Great-grandmother Viola got one house due to marriage, but she bought the other house with funds from the U.S. military because her brother served in World War II, and he jumped from a plane but his parachute did not open. This resulted in his death while serving our nation.

I don't know what else Great-grandmother Viola bought with that money, and I am not sure how much she received. She might have bought shoes, clothes, and hats or other material things, but what is so powerful to me is that she wanted to set up her family for future prosperity by giving them property, even during a time in U.S. history that was not favorable for women—let alone women of color—concerning them managing their own finances. Keep in mind, The Fair Housing Act, which protected homebuyers, owners, and renters from discrimination based on race, sex, religion, national origin, and disabilities, was not passed until 1968. In the 1940s, my Great-grandmother Viola was a trailblazer!

Here's her impact: One of my uncles was able to live in one house *mortgage free,* and the other house became the homestead, which was also *mortgage free,* and my grandparents, my mom, and her other siblings lived there. And even until this day, the legacy of one of the houses is still blessing some family members with *mortgage-free* living.

Let me also interject that Grandmother Mamie (Great-grandmother Viola's daughter) also inherited a house from someone whom she and my aunts took care of. Grandmother Mamie was a schoolteacher and then became a stay-at-home mom when she and Granddaddy Elton started having children. Grandmother Mamie would joke and say, "I don't have a job, but I have three houses!" She had the two houses passed down from Great-grandmother Viola and the other house she inherited.

There was something special about that generation. They had half of the conveniences we have, but they were more prosperous and left more to the next generation in many ways.

"A good person leaves an inheritance for their children' s children..."

— Proverbs 13:22

Granny—Grandmother Addie (Paternal)

My dad's mom is Grandmother Addie whom we call Granny. She lived in Newnan, Georgia. Granny went from assisting my grandfather, Mallory Carvin (M.C.), as a sharecropper to doing domestic work outside the home to providing for the daily needs of her family (with eight children) within the household—Granny was a hard worker. As a young child, Granny joined Wesley Chapel A.M.E. Church, eventually serving faithfully as superintendent of the Sunday school, president of the usher board, a missionary, church secretary, and a dedicated member.

Granny was fondly remembered for her gardening (including her snake bite), her good home cooking and canning (particularly the biscuits, fried green tomatoes, and pear preserves), and her beautiful quilting, which merited an article in the *Newnan Times Herald*. I have one of her beautiful quilts.

Here's what else is powerful about my granny: She had forty-plus acres of land in rural Georgia. Yes, you read that correctly, forty acres (I never heard that she got a mule!*). She and my grandfather M.C. were able to give their children (and subsequently grandchildren) acres and acres of land. Granny gave them land *while* she was living. Her children did not have to wait until her death to inherit the land. So, two of my aunts built homes and raised families on their section of the land along with my Granny and Granddad's house. The other siblings maintained their ownership of their portion of the land, which to this date, has not left the Mitchell family.

In 2010, I was blessed by this legacy to have inherited five acres of this family land, which I still own and pay taxes on every year. The value of this land has doubled in the last five years.

I can't imagine what Granny experienced being born in 1914 and working as a sharecropper, but I believe Granny and Granddad wanted their legacy to be prosperous and flourish far beyond their years and imagination.

"These trees which he plants, and under whose shade he shall never sit, he loves them for themselves, and for the sake of his children and his children's children, who are to sit beneath the shadow of their spreading boughs."

Forty Acres and a Mule

— Hyacinthe Loyson, French preacher and
theologian, sermon quote, 1866

––––––––––

"Forty acres and a mule" refers to a promise made to formerly enslaved African Americans during the Reconstruction era in the United States following the Civil War. The phrase symbolizes the idea of providing land and resources to formerly enslaved individuals as a form of reparations for centuries of slavery and oppression. After the Civil War, General William T. Sherman issued Special Field Orders No. 15, which allocated confiscated Confederate land along the southeastern coast for the settlement of freed slaves. Each family was to receive up to forty acres of land and, in some cases, a mule to help with agricultural labor. However, this promise was short-lived. President Andrew Johnson overturned Sherman's order, returning the land to its former Confederate owners. The phrase forty acres and a mule *has since become a powerful symbol of the unfulfilled promises and injustices faced by African Americans in their struggle for equality and justice in the United States.*

––––––––

I should mention that neither side of my family has millionaires (yet) or anyone who you might identify as rich. At best, my grandparents on both sides would be classified as middle class. But it was clear that they were rich and prosperous in their foresight, impact, and in their actions. I am incredibly blessed to be a part of their legacy, and I hope they are proud. I regret that I did not learn more about them and their younger years while they were still living.

My maternal and paternal grandparents remind me of the song by Elevation Worship called "The Blessing," featuring Cody Carnes and Kari Jobe. The song talks about God's favor being on your family and your children's children.

As I continued thinking about where prosperity and a prosperous mindset has shown up in my life, I thought about my mom, Bettye! If you are connected to me on social media, you will consistently see her comments and constant support of anything that I post or share! She so graciously pours love over everything that I do. I realize that everyone does not have that experience and support system, and I am highly fortunate for that.

Bigger and greater than that, my mom is a retired registered nurse of almost forty years. She went from being a medical technician to a licensed practical nurse (LPN) to a registered nurse (RN) and an RNIII by retirement. Oh, and she obtained her LPN and RN licenses while married, raising two kids, and working fulltime!

My mom worked and specialized in open-heart patients, cardiovascular intensive care unit, oncology, intensive care unit, critical care unit, and finally post-anesthesia care unit.

One day, we were driving to Georgia to visit family for Thanksgiving, and we started talking about her job. My mom said, "I *love* my job!...I *love* nursing!" I was probably in my forties at this point, and it struck me and stuck with me. Keep in mind that she has been in the field of nursing since I was in elementary school. I never heard her say that before even though I knew she was an amazing nurse, according to the doctors and her patients. When she eventually retired, it was very emotional and filled with tears because she would still be working if I let her! What a blessing to have an almost forty-year career in a field that you loved. My sister, Kym, and I were blessed to have a parent who found her passion and purpose in her work or as her former employer, St. Mary's Hospital, called it, *the ministry of nursing*.

There are so many people who hate their job or hate the work environment they are in. When an adult dislikes their job, it can have a ripple effect on their personal life and family dynamics. Here's a look at some of the key impacts:

- **Emotional and Physical Health:** Job dissatisfaction can lead to stress, anxiety, and depression. This stress can manifest physically, causing issues like headaches, fatigue, and worsened chronic conditions. The emotional and physical toll not only affects the individual but can also strain family relationships.
- **Work-Life Balance:** Disliking a job can make it difficult to leave work issues at the office, leading to problems with work-life balance. This might result in less quality time with family, which can affect relationships and overall family happiness.
- **Financial Stress:** If the job dissatisfaction is linked to inadequate pay or fear of job loss, this can lead to financial stress. Financial insecurity can heighten tensions within the family, impacting decisions about savings and future planning.
- **Modeling for Children:** Children often look up to their parents as role models. Witnessing a parent consistently unhappy with their work can influence their own perceptions of work and career, possibly leading them to normalize job dissatisfaction.

This list could go on to other impacts, but I wanted to stop here at the last impact on children. You might not be able to buy everything your family wants or go on the types of vacations you see others going on or live in the biggest house, but there is no greater impact a parent can have on a child and adult children other than to be happy and do the things and work they like and love. Let's not forget, prosperity can also be found in the passion for your work.

If you find yourself in the place of disliking your career, I challenge you to pinpoint what exactly about the job makes you unhappy. Is it the work environment, the tasks, the hours, or maybe the relationships with colleagues or directors? Understanding the specific issues can help in formulating a solution. Sometimes, simple changes at your current job can make a big difference. Consider talking to your supervisor about modifying your role, reducing workload, flexing your hours, or addressing interpersonal conflicts. It's surprising how often employers are willing to provide accommodations to retain valued employees. If your current field is not fulfilling, think about transitioning to a different one, and/or starting a business (read my chapter in *Prepare for Purpose*—"The Exit Strategy"—available on Amazon and Barnes and Noble). This may require more substantial planning, but it can ultimately lead to greater personal satisfaction.

God is so faithful to me to have the blood of prosperous people running in my veins. Do I have everything I want? No. Has my business reached the revenue levels it could? No. Have I hired the team I want? No. Has my personal life gone in the direction I thought? No. But here is the thing, God has blessed me beyond measure with life, freedom, impact, health, flexibility of schedule, and strength. As a full-time entrepreneur since February 2018 (without a rich husband, well...no husband as of the printing of this book!), I have prospered in my endeavors. Even through the COVID-19 pandemic, my business and I are still standing.

I began thinking about what has helped me advance. Here's what came to mind:

1. Prayer
2. Affirmations and Declarations

Prayer

When I first left my twenty-five-year career at Capital One Bank, I started a new morning routine. One part of this routine was prayer.

Some kind of way, I ran across Kachelle Kelly on social media and picked up a copy of her book, *Boss Women Pray–31 Prayers to Increase Your Success and Spirit* (*The Comprehensive Prayer Guide for Entrepreneurs and Women in Leadership*). Among other prayers, she had a morning prayer and an evening prayer. I started reading/saying those prayers most days.

Yes, I could have just talked to God in my own words, but these prayers gave language to me specifically as an entrepreneur and woman in leadership. For example, one part of her prayer says, "Let my social media be effective today." Another line said, "Go before me in my meetings and speaking engagements to grow my business." Wow! Sometimes we overcomplicate things and think that we need really eloquent words when we talk to God. He just wants a conversation with you. That's prayer.

So, I decided to write a few prayers for you, and perhaps they will be impactful and help you flourish like Kachelle Kelly's book did for me. You can say them daily or as needed. Put a bookmark on this page!

- Prayer for Men
- Prayer for Women
- Prayer for Entrepreneurs
- Prayer for Your Marketing
- Prayer for Single Women Leaders
- Prayer for Career Shifts

Prayer for Men

Dear God,

As I rise each day, I place my family, my career, and my leadership roles into Your hands. Grant me the wisdom to lead with compassion and the strength to support those who depend on me. Bless my family with unity and love, and let my home be a sanctuary of peace and encouragement.

In my career, provide me with opportunities to excel and the clarity to make decisions that propel me forward. Put the right people in my corner who will go to bat for me. I recognize Your grace in every task I undertake.

As a leader, give me vision and focus. Help me to inspire others with my actions and words, leading by example. May I foster environments where people feel valued and empowered.

Protect me from distractions and guide me in paths that lead to good success. Let my life be a testament to Your faithfulness, as I seek to grow in all areas entrusted to me.

Bless me with health, wealth, access, happiness, and the courage to face life with confidence, knowing You are with me at every step.

In Jesus' name, I pray. Amen.

Prayer for Women

Dear God,

Today, I stand before You ready to embrace the prosperity and advancement You have set before me. Bless me with the vision to recognize opportunities where others see obstacles, and grant me the courage to move forward, even on paths less traveled.

Give me the wisdom and grace to build and nurture networks that will support and strengthen my endeavors and the grace to lead with integrity and compassion. May I prosper not only in wealth, but also in wisdom and wellness.

Open wide the doors of advancement, leading me to higher ground in both my career and personal life. Equip me and those connected to me with the tools to excel, the resilience to overcome setbacks, and the spirit to persevere through challenges.

Let my actions reflect my faith in You and in the bright future You have promised and planned for me. May I inspire others not only by what I achieve but also by my character. Bless me with a legacy of breakthroughs and a life marked by Your favor and joy.

In Jesus' name, I pray. Amen.

Prayer for Entrepreneurs

Dear God,

Today, as I navigate the path of entrepreneurship, I seek Your guidance and wisdom. Bless me with clarity to see my path clearly and the boldness to pursue it, even amid uncertainty. Infuse my decisions with integrity and foresight, and let my endeavors be met with Your divine favor and revenue.

Strengthen me to overcome challenges with resilience and flexibility, turning every setback into a forward stride. Let my business serve as a channel of prosperity and profit for myself, my family and my current and future team.

Inspire me with a spirit of innovation and a mindset geared toward continual growth. Make me a leader who enables confidence and a collaborator who builds lasting connections. May my services and products glorify You and serve as a beacon of hope and inspiration to others.

Grant me the courage to embrace new ideas and strategies, and provide me the peace of knowing You are with me in every step. Prosper my marketing, business development, contracts, proposals, and sales, Lord, as I operate in excellence and seek to make a positive impact in the world.

In Jesus' name, I pray. Amen.

Prayer for Your Marketing

Dear God,

I come to you in faith. You see the dreams I have, the aspirations that drive me, and the vision I seek to bring to fruition through my business. Lord, as I focus on my marketing, I ask for your divine instruction, guidance, visiblity and favor.

Grant me the creativity to weave captivating brand stories and compelling content messages that resonate deeply with my target audience. Layer my marketing strategies and marketing plan with innovation and insight, that they may stand out through the noise of the marketplace.

Bless my efforts with an abundance of opportunities, leads, sales, revenue, profit and prosperity. Open doors for collaborations, partnerships, and connections that will increase the visibility and credibility of my business and brand to new heights. May every marketing tactic I undertake yield a rich harvest of success, bringing forth increased sales, customer engagement, and profitability.

Guard my heart from the whispers of doubt and discouragement, reminding me that with You, all things are possible. Strengthen my mindset in periods of slow sales, and inspire me with fresh ideas and strategies.

Above all, may my marketing efforts attract my ideal clients and ideal contracts.

I trust that you are faithful to fulfill your promises and guide me every step of the way.

In Jesus' name, I pray. Amen.

Prayer for Single Women Leaders

Dear God,

As I begin this day, I seek Your wisdom and strength to lead with courage and grace. As a single woman, empower me to manage the responsibilities before me with grace, clarity, and purpose. Bless my path as I navigate both my personal and professional life with independence and confidence.

Surround me with supportive relationships that uplift and inspire me. Help me to build and maintain connections that enrich my life and strengthen me.

In my leadership roles, grant me the vision to see opportunities for growth and the bold confidence to pursue them despite the challenges. Let my influence be a source of inspiration, and let my decisions be a reflection of Your love and justice.

Protect me from discouragement and loneliness, and wrap your love around me. Provide me with the discernment to recognize when to lead versus when to listen. Remind me that You know the plans You have for me and remind me that You are the author of time. There is nothing missing and nothing broken in my life.

As I impact the world around me, let my life be a testament to Your goodness and mercy. May my life encourage other women to embrace their own paths with boldness and faith.

In Jesus' name, I pray. Amen.

Prayer for Career Shifts

Dear God,

As I stand at this crossroads, ready to switch up my career, I'm calling on You for some guidance. Light up my path with Your wisdom, and show me the moves that match my skills and what I'm passionate about. Give me the insight to know the right steps to take and the guts, courage, and grace to jump on the opportunities that come my way.

Allow me to recognize the assets and value I bring to the table. Bring people into my life who will lift me up and push me forward, keeping me strong in what I believe and who I am as I chase down this new path.

Calm my nerves, Lord, and replace that stress with Your peace, reminding me that You've got a bigger plan in store for me. Stabilize me when things get rocky, knowing that the best changes don't happen overnight.

Let this career shift not just boost my own life, but also let me be a blessing to others through the work I'm heading into.

Help me to remain steadfast in my values and true to myself as I pursue this new direction. Ease my anxieties and replace them with your peace, knowing that You have a plan for my life that is greater than any I could envision. I embrace this career shift with ease.

In Jesus' name, I pray. Amen.

Affirmations and Declarations

Similar to prayer, I use and say affirmations and/or declarations. I really got into this when I picked up a copy of a workbook by Robin M. Ware, CMP, called *How to Make Your Inbox Your Cash Box —Strategies that Successful Entrepreneurs Use to Make Money Online While they Sleep, Pray and Hustle*. In this workbook, she gives practical business tips and advice, but there was a two- to three-page declaration that knocked my socks off! I pulled out my phone and clicked on the voice memo app and read aloud the declaration. Every other week or so, I click the voice memo, and I listen to myself saying that declaration. There is power in your voice.

> For verily I say unto you, That whosoever shall **say** unto this mountain, Be thou removed, and be thou cast into the sea; and shall not doubt in his heart, but shall believe that those things which he **saith** shall come to pass; he shall have whatsoever he **saith**.
>
> — Mark 11:23 (KJV; emphasis added)

What is an Affirmation or Declaration?

Affirmations and declarations are like your personal cheerleaders, guiding you toward a mindset for success and self-growth.

Think of affirmations as positive, uplifting statements you tell yourself to foster belief in your abilities and goals. They're like little whispers of encouragement, reminding you of the strengths you possess and the success that's within reach. For instance, saying "I am full of confidence and ready for success" serves as a mental reinforcement that can shape your actions and outlook.

Why They Work

1. Shifts Your Mindset: Both affirmations and declarations can transform a doubtful mind into a powerhouse of positivity and determination. This mental shift is crucial because it fuels your drive to achieve big things.

2. Sparks Behavioral Changes: As you start believing in the positive messages you feed yourself, your behavior naturally aligns with these thoughts. If you consistently affirm your leadership qualities, for instance, you'll likely find yourself stepping up more as a leader.

3. *Boosts Performance:* There's real evidence showing that positive self-talk through affirmations can elevate performance across different areas of life—from sports to your love life to public speaking —by enhancing focus and self-belief.

4. *Benefits Your Brain:* Regularly engaging in affirmations can actually rewire your brain through neuroplasticity (the brain's ability to absorb information and evolve to manage new challenges), making positive thinking a more automatic state.

Though affirmations and declarations are powerful tools, they aren't magic wands. Their effectiveness hinges on your belief in them and the consistent action you take toward your goals.

So, I decided to write a few affirmations and declarations for you.

Assignment: Take out your phone, turn on your voice memo, and record yourself saying your favorite affirmations/declarations from this list of forty. Listen to your recording every week.

Affirmations and Declarations

1. I am destined to prosper.
2. Abundance and blessings overflow in every area of my life.
3. I declare that prosperity is my birthright.
4. Financial breakthroughs, career advancements, and opportunities come easy to me.
5. I am resilient, resourceful, and I receive all the blessings He has for me.
6. I sow seeds of generosity, kindness, and love, knowing that as I give, I also receive abundantly.
7. My actions align with God's will, and my prosperity multiplies exponentially.
8. Today, I speak victory over every setback, setup, and hindrance.

9. I am anointed to prosper, blessed to succeed, and empowered to live a life of abundance and fulfillment.
10. I deserve prosperity in all areas of my life, and I embrace abundance with open arms.
11. Every day, I attract opportunities that lead me closer to my goals and dreams.
12. I am confident in my abilities and trust that I am capable of achieving great success.
13. My mind is a magnet for positive energy, drawing prosperity, and abundance into my life effortlessly.
14. I release all limiting beliefs and embrace a mindset of abundance and possibility.
15. I am grateful for the abundance that surrounds me, and I celebrate every achievement along my journey.
16. I am worthy of financial prosperity, and I attract wealth and abundance with ease.
17. I am fearless and unafraid as all my dreams manifest.
18. I embrace this week with ease.
19. Every seed I sow yields a good harvest.
20. I belong in every room I walk in.
21. Good opportunities are looking for me.
22. My actions align with my goals, and I am committed to taking consistent steps toward my vision of success.
23. I radiate confidence, positivity, and resilience, attracting opportunities wherever I go.
24. I am the architect of my destiny, and I create a life filled with joy, love, abundance, and fulfillment.
25. I cultivate love, understanding, and compassion in all my relationships.
26. Every day, I communicate openly and honestly with my loved ones, nurturing trust and harmony within my family.
27. I prioritize quality time with my family, creating cherished memories and strengthening our bonds of love and unity.

28. I resolve conflicts peacefully and constructively, fostering a harmonious and supportive environment for my family to thrive.
29. I honor the unique strengths and perspectives of each family member, embracing uniqueness and celebrating our collective growth.
30. I cherish every moment we share together, knowing that our connection is a precious gift.
31. I am destined to prosper in my business endeavors.
32. The Lord has planted seeds of success within me, and I reap a bountiful harvest of prosperity and health.
33. I declare that my business is ordained for greatness.
34. Financial abundance, strategic partnerships, and exponential growth happen every day.
35. I am anchored in the promise of God's provision.
36. My business is resilient, adaptable, and poised for long-term success.
37. I embed seeds of innovation, excellence, and integrity in my business practices.
38. My clients are blessed by my products and services.
39. My brand attracts loyal customers and repeat buyers.
40. From operations to marketing, from product development to customer service, I lead my business to unprecedented levels of success and revenue.

If you do the voice note assignment, send me an email and let me know! Send the message to sharvette@mitchellproductions.biz.

Here we are 5,000-plus words later for a chapter that I almost did not write. I think the moral of the story is that we all can look back and see that we have prospered in some area or that prosperity is around us within reach. I hope this chapter was a reminder of that.

Forty Acres and a Mule

Beloved, I wish above all things that thou mayest prosper and be in health, even as thy soul prospereth.

— 3 John 2

Meet the Author | Sharvette Mitchell

Sharvette Mitchell is more than a business leader and marketing consultant; she's The Platform Builder®. Her vision, ingenuity, and extensive twenty-five-year background in corporate America at Capital One Bank, coupled with a bachelor of science in marketing from Virginia Commonwealth University, have crystallized her reputation as a foremost authority in the marketing landscape.

Sharvette's unique approach, encapsulated in her trademarked framework The Platform Builder®, has become a beacon for small businesses seeking to amplify their brand. By honing their visibility, marketing, and branding strategies, she has enabled numerous businesses to generate more revenue, achieve growth, and establish increased brand recognition.

Her one-on-one consulting, innovative group coaching programs, engaging speaking/training, and live conferences/summits have been applauded for their effectiveness and creativity. As a marketing consultant, her insight into consumer behavior and online market trends has made her an indispensable asset for growing businesses aiming to elevate their brand presence in the competitive market.

Sharvette's acclaim extends to being featured in prestigious publications such as *Yahoo! Finance, AARP, Huffington Post, HOPE* magazine, CBNation, and *Sista Sense* Magazine, where her thoughts on marketing and branding are often sought. Her appearances on CBS 6 *Monday Motivation*, CBS 6 *Virginia This Morning*, The CW Network, and Comcast Cable showcase her as a thought leader.

Her certifications as Women Owned Small Business (WOSB) with the U.S. Small Business Administration and The Small, Women-owned, and Minority-owned Business (SWaM) by the Virginia Department of Small Business and Supplier Diversity demonstrate her commitment to inclusivity in the business landscape. Moreover, as an International Coaching Federation (ICF) Professional Certified Life Coach, Sharvette embodies a blend of coaching and influential leadership.

Since 2008, *The Sharvette Mitchell Radio Show,* with more than 745 episodes, has been a platform for marketing insights, powerful conversations, and interviews, resonating with listeners and viewers across multiple audio and live-streaming platforms. Sharvette is a past recipient of the *ACHI* magazine's Radio Personality of the Year Award.

A prolific author, Sharvette is behind six impactful book collaborations, including *PROPEL, POUR, PURSUE, PEARLS, Prepare for PURPOSE,* and *Positioned to PIVOT.* These works further illustrate her passion for guiding others to pursue their dreams and document their transformational stories or intellectual property.

Her previous role on the board of directors of James River Writers and current volunteer role with International Christian Ministries, Inc., attests to her contributions to the community and her peers.

Whether guiding a small business to marketing success, delivering powerful training, or redefining a brand's identity, Sharvette's strategic mind and marketing expertise stand as a testament to what can be achieved with strategy, consistency, and leadership.

Learn more at www.Mitchell-Productions.com and www.PlatformBuilder.biz.

Epilogue
A Mouth Full
Bishop Gale LeGrand Williams

Keep this Book of the Law always on your lips; meditate on it day and night, so that you may be careful to do everything written in it. Then you will be prosperous and successful.

— Joshua 1:8 (NIV 1984)

These were the instructions God gave to Joshua. Moses, the great leader, had just died, and Joshua was selected to replace him. I'm sure Joshua felt insecure, maybe a little fearful, and God knew Joshua needed instructions on what to do for his new assignment.

God starts by saying, *"Do not let this word of the law depart from your mouth."* God wanted Joshua to have a mouth full of His Word. Have you heard people say, "You have said a mouthful?" That means what you have said is important, meaningful, and truthful. That's what God's Word is—it's important, it's meaningful, and it's truth. What is your mouth full of?

God promised Joshua prosperity and good success if he kept his mouth full of His Word. People of God, we have to be careful with our words. Proverbs 18:21 in The Message Bible says *"words kill, words give life; they're either poison or fruit—you choose."* Jesus said in Matthew 15:11 (NLV) *"It is not what goes into a man's mouth that makes his mind and heart sinful. It is what comes out of a man's mouth that makes him sinful."* It's the words that are coming out of our mouths that bring us blessings or curses, prosperity or failure.

Then God tells Joshua to be sure to meditate on my words, which means to spend time thinking about the Word of God and what the words mean to you and for your life, because if God's Word is not in our minds, they will never come out of our mouths. God said when we speak His Word, we will have prosperity and good success. What is God saying to us about prosperity and good success?

1. God Wants Us to Prosper.

The Hebrew word for prosperity is *prä sperǝdē,* which means to advance. It means comfort, peace, wealth, good health, and deliverance. Do not let anyone tell you that God doesn't want you to prosper. Psalm 35:27 (AMPC) says God takes pleasure in the prosperity of His servants. Prosperity is God's plan for all His people. God's desire is for us to prosper. God is happy when we prosper. This does not mean He is standing on the corner handing out cars, boats, and hundred-dollar bills. Prosperity is more than money and stuff. Do not limit your definition of prosperity to money. There are many people in this world with money and no peace, money and bad health, and money with holes in their pockets, which means they make the money, but as soon as they get it, it's gone. We keep trying to figure out how we can be prosperous, but the secret to true prosperity is simple: It is God's Word in our minds and in our mouths.

2. God Gives Us Good Success.

God didn't just say Joshua would be successful. God said Joshua would have good success. Good success means we allow God to work all things together for us. If God says there is good success, then there must be a success that is not good. Anything we achieve that leaves us frustrated, tired, angry, arrogant, selfish, depressed, and isolated is not good success, no matter how many benefits may come with it. Sure, you got the promotion, but you can't get any sleep from stress. Yes, you got the man or woman that you wanted, but you have no peace. You got the house or car, but it is a money pit, and it's draining your finances. We have to surrender to God's plans; even when those plans are not our plans. Good success requires knowing God's Word and trusting God with our outcome. God said meditate on His Word and keep it in your mouth, and if you do this, you will succeed, and that success will be good.

3. Our Words Have Power.

I think some of us have been in church so long that we have forgotten the power we have as people of God. Just think about the words you have spoken in the last twenty-four hours. What have you said this morning—just today—that should not have been said? Maybe it was a criticism of yourself or words of doubt to yourself that didn't need to be said, or maybe it was a negative word to someone because you felt you had the authority to say it.

Matthew 12:37 in The Message Bible says, "*Let me tell you something: Every one of these careless words is going to come back to haunt you. There will be a time of Reckoning. Words are powerful; take them seriously. Words can be your salvation. Words can also be your damnation.*"

Or maybe we are like Peter, when he cursed at the woman who asked him if he was one of Jesus' followers. Matthew 26:74 (TLB) says,

"Peter began to curse and swear. 'I don't even know the man,' he said. And immediately the cock crowed."

Some of us are standing with our hands up in praise in the sanctuary and cussing in the car. We walk out of church speaking blessings to everyone, and we get on the highway and someone cuts us off—you know what I'm talking about—and then flows the cussing.

James 3:9–10 (CEV) says, *"My dear friends, with our tongues we speak both praises and curses. We praise our Lord and Father, and we curse people who were created to be like God, and this isn't right."*

Our words have power—the power to bless and the power to tear down. We have to watch our words. It is so important that we speak the Word of God in faith and do not speak contrary or foolish words. Don't confess the Word of God in one breath and speak doubt the next.

Hebrews 10:23 reminds us that we are to hold fast to our confession of faith, without wavering, because God who has promised us is faithful.

In this day and season in which we are living, we need to keep our minds and our mouths full of the Word of God, over ourselves, our families, our communities, and over this nation. Saints, we have to grow up. Paul said in 1 Corinthians 13:11, when I became an adult, I set aside childish ways.

We all want the blessings of God. We want to prosper, and God wants us to prosper, and He has prescribed in His Word how we can all prosper and have good success. Say what God says. If you are sick, say, *By the stripes of Jesus, I am healed.* If your money is funny, and you are in need, say, *I may not have the finances I need right now, but Jesus will provide for me according to His riches in glory.*

If you are tired of living in chaos, speak peace over your life, speak peace over your home. Jesus said He has left His peace with us. We have a legacy of peace, so speak peace. Jesus spoke to the storm and said, "Peace be still," and it did.

Joshua may have been fearful when God spoke to him in Chapter 1, because he witnessed all that God did through Moses, watching Moses hold out a stick and seeing the waters part and become dry land, which could have been intimidating, but after a while, by the time we get to Chapter 10, after Joshua understood the power of speaking God's Word, Joshua spoke and the sun and the moon stood still, and God gave Israel victory over their enemies. And the Bible says there has never been a day like that before or since.

God has a "never been before or since day" for each of us. We just have to keep our mouths full of His Word.

God's desire was for Joshua to prosper, to gain victory over every obstacle and to be successful in all of his tasks, and that's God's desire for each of us. We have to program our spirit for success. Speak the Word of God until it comes.

God does not want us broke or broken, sick or complacent. Jesus said He came that we might have life and life more abundantly, so we cannot blame God if we are living less than His best for us. God's Word comes alive when we put it in our mouths!

Speak God's promises over your life.

Keep your mind and your mouth full of God's Word.

Then you will be prosperous, and then you will have good success.

Meet the Author | Bishop Gale LeGrand Williams

Bishop Gale LeGrand Williams is a native of Norfolk, Virginia, and the president and founder of Entrusted Connections Ministry, Incorporated. Entrusted Connections Ministry, Incorporated (ECM) is a State of Virginia 501(c)(3) organization established in 2007 by Bishop Gale. It serves the community through services, events, activities, and resources that will help wherever there is a need.

ECM is dedicated to bringing health and wholeness to those who are simply trying to "fill in the cracks" in the broken seasons of their lives.

She is the president and chief executive officer of Entrusted Strategic Management Solutions Incorporated (ESMSI), a U. S. Small Business Administration–certified, woman-owned business management consulting company founded in 2004 in Woodbridge, Virginia.

Bishop Gale was selected to participate in the 2015 Goldman Sachs 10,000 Small Business Program, a $500 million initiative developed to provide selected U.S. entrepreneurs with an integrated program of practical business and management education, access to capital and business and management education, and access to capital and business support services.

Bishop Gale serves as second vice chairperson of the International Christian Ministries, Incorporated (ICM) board of directors in Richmond, Virginia, and also serves on the New Jerusalem International Christian Ministries board of directors. She is a member of the Joint College of African American Pentecostal Bishops in Cleveland, Ohio. Bishop Gale received the Princeton Theological Seminary's certificate in theology and ministry in January 2014.

She attended Delaware State College, majored in business administration, and later received a master's certificate in government contracting from George Washington University. During her career, she was appointed to the United States Senate as a legislative fellow for Senator Carl Levin.

To learn more about her, visit www.ec-ministry.com.